# NURSERY
## R · H · Y · M · E · S

### in
### CROSS STITCH

# NURSERY

## R · H · Y · M · E · S

### in
### CROSS STITCH

Dorothea Hall

MEREHURST

## ACKNOWLEDGEMENTS

*The author would like to offer her grateful thanks to the following people who helped with the cross stitching of projects in this book with such skill and enthusiasm: Gisela Banbury, Clarice Blakey, Caroline Davies, Christina Eustace, Janet Grey, Elizabeth Hall and Anne Whitbourn.*

*The publishers would like to thank Julie Hasler for her designs on pages 16-17, 24-25, 28-29, 36-37, 42-50, 53, 56-61, 64-65, 68, 72, 76, 84, 88 and 112-117, and for her help with the designs on pages 12-13, 33, 78-79, 92-93 and 96-97.*

*The publishers would also like to thank The Monogrammed Linen Shop, 68 Walton Street, London SW3, and Thomas Goode & Co, 19 South Audley Street, London W1Y 6BN, for kindly supplying linen and china on pages 34 and 110.*

Published 1991 by Merehurst Limited
Ferry House, 51-57 Lacy Road, Putney, London SW15 1PR

Reprinted 1992

© Copyright 1991 Merehurst Limited
ISBN 1 85391 243 3

A catalogue record for this book is available from the British Library.

Project Editor: Polly Boyd
Edited by Diana Brinton
Designed by Maggie Aldred
Photography by Di Lewis (pages 34-35, 110-111 by Stewart Grant)
Illustrations by John Hutchinson
Typesetting by Maron Graphics Limited
Colour separation by Fotographics Limited, UK – Hong Kong
Printed in Italy by New Interlitho, S.p.A., Milan

*Merehurst is the leading publisher of craft books and has an excellent range of titles to suit all levels. Please send to the address above for our free catalogue, stating the title of this book.*

# CONTENTS

| | |
|---|---|
| Introduction | 8 |
| Drinks Tray | 11 |
| Nightdress Case | 15 |
| Lacy Lavender Sachets | 19 |
| Fringed Place Mats and Napkins | 22 |
| Corded Cushion | 27 |
| Trim Bookmarks | 30 |
| Tea-Time Tray | 35 |
| Nursery-Rhyme Patchwork Quilt | 38 |
| Afternoon-Tea Cloth | 55 |
| Birthday Greetings Cards | 62 |
| Miniature Pictures | 67 |
| Pretty Pincushions | 70 |
| Coffee Time Companions | 75 |
| Christmas Greetings Cards | 83 |
| A Child's Picture | 87 |
| Bordered Pictures | 90 |
| Fringed Guest Towel | 95 |
| Victorian-Style Footstool | 99 |
| Tied-On Pillow Cover | 103 |
| Traditional Dressing-Table Set | 107 |
| Lace-Edged Cushions | 110 |
| Alphabet | 116 |
| Border Designs | 118 |
| Basic Equipment | 119 |
| Basic Skills | 121 |
| Conversion Chart | 126 |
| Index and Suppliers | 128 |

# INTRODUCTION

The tremendous feeling of satisfaction and pleasure we experience in embroidering and making a project – whether it is a quilt for the nursery or a simple bookmark for a friend – is borne out by the growing enthusiasm for cross stitch and the general revival of interest in traditional domestic crafts. The projects in this book, all of which are based on old nursery rhymes, include some which are suitable for beginners as well as others that are more challenging and are designed for experienced embroiderers.

Cross stitch occupies a special place among embroidery crafts, for it was at one time a much-practised activity. Young girls were taught to embroider by working immensely detailed samplers in cross stitch, learning to embroider all kinds of complex designs, repeating border patterns, letters and numerals with great dexterity and charm, before progressing to other household items, such as hand-towels, napkins, table-cloths and pillow covers.

While researching nursery rhymes for this book, I have found a similar charm and variety in the beautifully illustrated verses handed down from past generations. In fact, charm played a major part in the inspiration of the book, since so much came initially from the nursery rhymes themselves and from the equally delightful illustrations. What child, for example, could resist the magic of 'Hey, diddle diddle, the cat and the fiddle, the cow jumped over the moon', and what mother would not respond to 'Little maiden, better tarry; time enough next year to marry'. Evocative verses such as these, combined with the artistry of A. Rackham and R. Caldecott, for example, have kept me thoroughly inspired and amused from beginning to end.

The choice of projects proved tantalizing, as did matching a particular nursery rhyme to a

*Some of the most striking illustrations, and the most adaptable for cross stitch embroidery, are those of R. Caldecott, whose sensitive line and use of flat, subtle colour is clearly inspirational.*

*Not all nursery rhyme designs need be of large proportions – indeed, the smallest motifs can be equally charming (and much quicker to embroider), as seen here in the lavender sachets and the Little Boy Blue pillow cover.*

project. However, it would be a simple operation to convert many of the designs to suit your personal needs. Take the miniature pictures, for example, or the traditional dressing table set; these designs could quite easily be mounted as greetings cards or pincushions. And the tray designs could equally well be used as pictures or cushion covers. The child's patchwork quilt, embroidered with verses of twelve popular nursery rhymes, is in itself a miniature record of some of our best-loved verses. And what would make handier bed-time reading? Indeed the quilt might even become a teaching aid to encourage reading skills! As an alternative to a quilt, however, you may prefer to embroider the verses (or any of the other verses given in the book) and stitch them together to make a washable fabric book. With a little pre-planning, you could have immense fun adding borders of your choice, or using some of those given at the end of the book, to create further designs of your own. Using the alphabet, also given at the end of the book, you can add initials to your embroidery or spell out a name to personalize your gifts. The combinations are endless.

In making these projects, I hope you experience the satisfaction and fun I have had in creating them; this will happen because cross stitch and our well-loved nursery rhymes have an enduring attraction and, hopefully, will continue to be cherished by generations to come.

*Dorothea Hall*

## BEFORE YOU BEGIN

Each project begins with a full list of the materials that you will require. Note that the measurements given for the embroidery fabric include a minimum of 3cm (1¼in) all around to allow for stretching it in a frame and preparing the edges.

A colour key for DMC stranded embroidery cotton is given with each chart. You will need to buy one skein of each colour mentioned, though you may use less. Where two or more skeins are needed this is mentioned in the main list of requirements. Each cross stitch colour is represented by a symbol, but backstitch (bks) colours are listed by number only. Where a backstitch number is followed by a star, you will need to buy that colour in addition to the others. All other backstitch colours are also used for cross stitching and will therefore be mentioned in the list against a symbol.

Should you wish to use Coats/Anchor or Madeira stranded embroidery cottons, refer to the conversion chart given at the back of the book.

To work from the charts, particularly those where several symbols are used in close proximity, some readers may find it helpful to have the chart enlarged so that the squares and symbols can be seen more easily. Many photocopying services will do this for a minimum charge.

When you begin to cross stitch, use the centre lines given on the chart and the basting threads on your fabric as reference points for counting the squares and threads to position your design accurately.

# DRINKS TRAY

When friends come to stay, what better way is there to say 'good night' than to share a bed-time drink on a tray you've embroidered yourself?

## COME OUT TO PLAY

Girls and boys come out to play,
The moon doth shine as bright as day;
Leave your supper, and leave your sleep,
And come with your playfellows into
the street.
Come with a whoop, come with a call,
Come with a good will or not at all.

### COME OUT TO PLAY ▲

| | | | |
|---|---|---|---|
| ⊖ | white (bks 926) | ● 3350 deep pink | ⊡ 831 brown |
| ÷ | 832 gold | = 598 blue (bks 926) | I 926 grey blue |
| ↑ | 225 flesh (bks 3354) | ◆ 733 olive | ◤ 924 dark grey blue |
| ✱ | 3354 pink | ↓ 731 dark olive | ○ 3024 light grey (bks 535) |
| | | S 422 buff | △ 535 dark grey |

# DRINKS TRAY

## YOU WILL NEED

For a tray measuring 33cm × 20.5cm
(13in × 8in) with a 28.5cm × 16cm
(11¼in × 6¼in) oval cut out:

*40cm × 30cm (16in × 12in) of cream evenweave
(Aida) fabric, 14 threads to 2.5cm (1in)
DMC stranded embroidery cotton in the colours
given in the panel shown opposite
No24 tapestry needle
33cm × 20.5cm (13in × 8in) of lightweight
iron-on interfacing
Oval wooden tray (for suppliers, see page 128)*

•

## THE EMBROIDERY

Begin by stretching the prepared fabric in an embroidery frame (see page 121). Then, following the colour key and chart, complete the cross stitching, using two strands of thread in the needle throughout. Remove the embroidery from the frame and, if necessary, steam press it on the wrong side. Do not remove the basting stitches at this stage.

## ASSEMBLING THE TRAY

Using a soft pencil, mark the mounting card (supplied with the tray) both ways along the centre.

Lay the embroidery face down on a clean surface. Centre the card over it, with the pencil lines and basting stitches matching, and lightly draw around the card outline, using the pencil. Remove the basting threads, carefully cut out the embroidery, and back it with the lightweight iron-on interfacing. Alternatively, trim the fabric to leave a 4cm (1½in) allowance, and run a gathering thread around 12mm (½in) away from the pencil line. Position the card and pull up the gathers evenly. Either lace across the back or secure the edges with masking tape.

Follow the manufacturer's instructions to complete the assembly of your tray.

# *N*IGHTDRESS CASE

Make this roomy bag to tuck
away your nightie or pyjamas for
the day. It is lightly padded and
finished with bows, and will sit
comfortably on top of the bed, as
soft as any pillow.

❖

### BAA-BAA BLACK SHEEP

Baa-baa black sheep, have you any wool?
Yes sir, yes sir, three bags full;
One for my master, one for my dame,
And one for the little boy who lives in
our lane.

**BAA-BAA BLACK SHEEP** ▲

| | | | |
|---|---|---|---|
| | ⊜ 742 orange | ‖ 948 flesh (bks 352) | ◣ 3053 sap green |
| | ◺ 729 gold | ↑ 3325 blue | ÷ 470 green |
| H white (bks 415) | ↓ 434 brown | ⊡ 322 dark blue | ◆ 935 dark green |
| ✕ 744 yellow | ✳ 352 pink | = 471 light green | S 415 light grey |

△ 317 grey
● 310 black

# NIGHTDRESS CASE

## YOU WILL NEED

For a nightdress case measuring 41cm × 30·5cm (16in × 12in):

*90cm × 46cm (1yd × 18in) of dusky pink evenweave fabric such as Lugana 403, 25 threads to 2.5cm (1in)*
*90cm × 46cm (1yd × 18in) of pale pink lawn for the lining*
*90cm × 46cm (1yd × 18in) of lightweight synthetic batting*
*115cm (1¼yds) of matching pink ribbon, 2cm (¾in) wide*
*DMC stranded embroidery cotton in the colours given in the panel on page 16*
*No26 tapestry needle*
*Matching sewing thread*

•

## THE EMBROIDERY

With the edges prepared, stretch the top fabric in an embroidery frame, see page 121. Baste the fold lines as shown in the diagram, and baste the positioning lines for the motif, following the chart given opposite. Then, referring to the colour key and the chart, complete the cross stitching, using two strands of thread in the needle throughout; use a single strand for the backstitching. Remove the fabric from the frame and steam press on the wrong side, if necessary.

## MAKING THE NIGHTDRESS CASE

Place the top fabric face down on a flat surface; carefully smooth the batting on top, and pin and baste. Trim the edges of the batting to clear the seam allowance all around and catch-stitch the edges of the batting to the seam allowance.

Make a single turning on the short edge (not the flap edge) of the front section and baste; 12mm (½in) seam allowances are used throughout. With right sides facing, fold up the front section, baste and machine stitch the side seams to form the pocket. Trim the corners and turn to the right side.

Make a single turning on the short edge of the

lining fabric and repeat as for the top fabric, but do not turn the pocket to the right side.

With right sides of the top fabric and lining together, baste and stitch around the flap, finishing just above the side seams. Trim the corners and turn the flap through to the right side. Slip the lining into the pocket and slipstitch the top edges together, easing the turning so that the stitching is on the inside. Remove the basting stitches.

Cut the ribbon into two equal lengths. Make two bows and catch-stitch them to the flap edge, as shown on the diagram.

## CUTTING LAYOUT

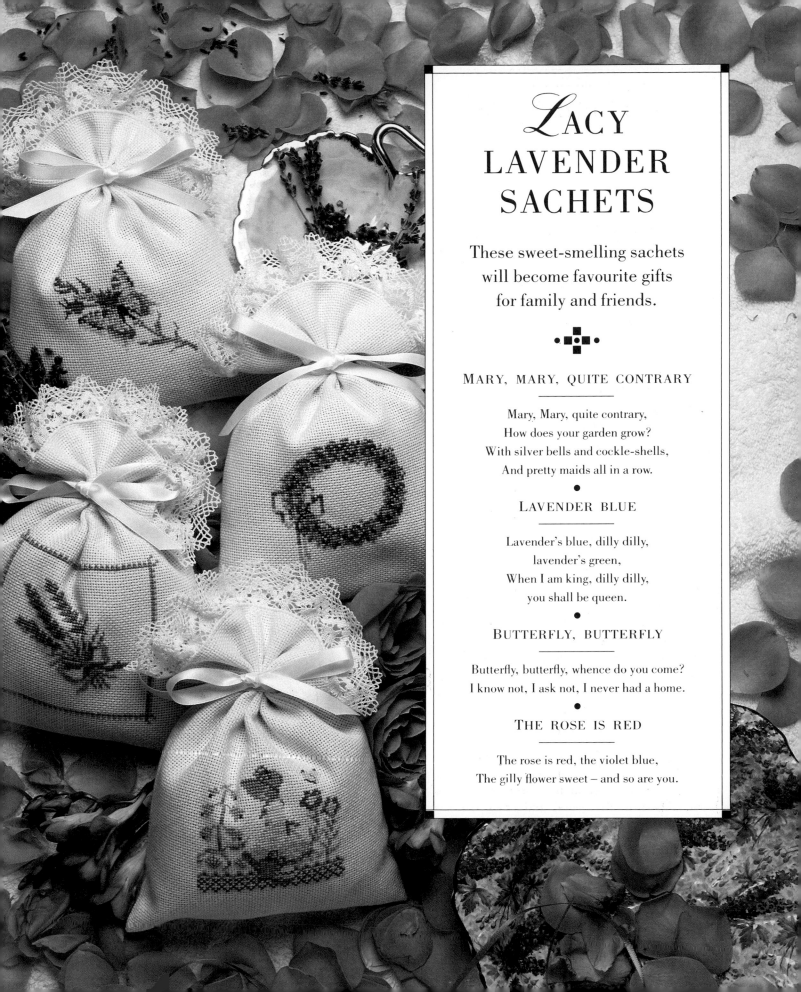

# Lacy
# LAVENDER
# SACHETS

These sweet-smelling sachets
will become favourite gifts
for family and friends.

❖

### MARY, MARY, QUITE CONTRARY

Mary, Mary, quite contrary,
How does your garden grow?
With silver bells and cockle-shells,
And pretty maids all in a row.

•

### LAVENDER BLUE

Lavender's blue, dilly dilly,
lavender's green,
When I am king, dilly dilly,
you shall be queen.

•

### BUTTERFLY, BUTTERFLY

Butterfly, butterfly, whence do you come?
I know not, I ask not, I never had a home.

•

### THE ROSE IS RED

The rose is red, the violet blue,
The gilly flower sweet – and so are you.

# LACY LAVENDER SACHETS

## YOU WILL NEED

For one sachet, with an overall measurement of
23cm × 15cm (9in × 6in):

*50cm × 20cm (20in × 8in) of white openweave*
*fabric, such as cotton Davosa or natural linen,*
*18 threads to 2.5cm (1in)*
*32.5cm (13in) of pre-gathered white lace trim,*
*4cm (1½in) wide*
*70cm (28in) of double-sided white satin ribbon,*
*1cm (⅜in) wide*
*DMC stranded embroidery cotton in the colours*
*given in the appropriate panel on pages 20, 21*
*No26 tapestry needle*
*Matching sewing thread*
*Sufficient lavender or pot pourri to fill the*
*sachet halfway*

•

## THE EMBROIDERY

To transfer the positioning lines to the embroidery,
fold the fabric widthways in half and mark this line
with a pin. Measure 8cm (3in) in from this point
and baste across. Baste the upright centre line.

With the fabric held in a hoop, follow the chart
and complete the motif, using two strands of thread
in the needle. Where several colours are required,
and to save time in starting and finishing, you may
prefer to keep two or three needles in use, pinning
them to the side when those particular colours are
not being used.

Remove the basting stitches and steam press the
finished embroidery on the wrong side.

## MAKING UP THE SACHET

With the wrong side facing out, fold the fabric
widthways in half; baste and machine stitch the
sides, taking a 2.5cm (1in) seam. If the edges have
frayed, check that the width of the sachet is 15cm
(6in). Trim the seam allowances to 12mm (½in),
and turn to the right side. Make a 4cm (1½in)
single turning on the top edge and baste.

Join the short edges of the lace trim, using a tiny
french seam. Pin and baste the trim to the inside
of the top edge and, working from the right side,
machine stitch in place, sewing close to the top
edge.

Half fill the sachet with lavender and tie the
ribbon twice around the top, finishing with the bow
in front.

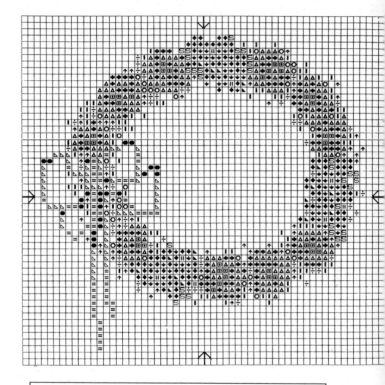

### THE ROSE IS RED ▲

| | | | |
|---|---|---|---|
| ‖ | 445 yellow | ↓ | 792 violet |
| △ | 3733 pink | = | 3761 turquoise |
| ✱ | 603 magenta | ÷ | 959 veridian green |
| ⊡ | 817 dark red | ⊆ | 943 dark green |
| ◆ | 341 pale blue | ∣ | 989 green |
| ◺ | 794 blue | ↑ | 471 olive |
| ● | 798 deep blue | ○ | 3051 dark olive |
| ◣ | 3609 mauve | | |

## BUTTERFLY, BUTTERFLY ▲

- ↑ 445 yellow
- ◣ 783 ochre
- I 721 orange
- ◆ 734 khaki (bks wing)
- ⊡ 602 pink
- ✳ 349 red
- △ 989 green
- ✦ 993 veridian green
- ○ 930 dark green blue
- S 340 light blue
- ● 792 dark blue
- △ 824 navy blue

## MARY, MARY ▲

- II white (bks bloomers 930, collar 794)
- ◇ 745 pale lemon (bks butterfly wing 783)
- ✕ 445 pale yellow
- △ 444 bright yellow
- ◆ 783 deep yellow
- ↑ 948 flesh (bks cockle shells 783)
- ⊡ 605 pink
- ● 603 deep pink
- ✳ 3705 red
- = 3761 pale blue
- ⊟ 3766 turquoise
- ✦ 930 slate grey (bks butterfly body)
- I 794 blue
- S 564 pale green
- △ 958 veridian green
- ÷ 3348 green
- ◣ 702 dark green
- ○ 3053 khaki

## LAVENDER BLUE ▶

- ✳ 224 pink
- ● 892 geranium
- ⊡ 340 violet
- △ 341 blue
- ✦ 368 green
- (bks stems)

# FRINGED PLACE MATS AND NAPKINS

Breakfast for two! Give a little personal touch to plain place mats and napkins by embroidering them with these exquisite corner motifs and finishing with a simple fringed hem.

### HICKETY, PICKETY

Hickety, pickety, my black hen,
She lays eggs for gentlemen;
Gentlemen come every day
To see what my black hen doth lay.

•

### HUMPTY DUMPTY

Humpty Dumpty sat on a wall
Humpty Dumpty had a great fall;
All the King's horses and all the King's men
Couldn't put Humpty Dumpty together again.

# FRINGED PLACE MATS AND NAPKINS

## YOU WILL NEED

For two place mats, each measuring
47cm × 33cm (18½in × 13in), and two napkins
each measuring 40.5cm (16in) square:

*90cm (1yd) of evenweave (Linda) fabric
84cm (33in) wide, 27 threads to 2.5cm (1in);
alternatively, prepared table mats can be purchased
from specialist suppliers (see page 128)
DMC stranded embroidery cotton in the colours
given in the panels
No26 tapestry needle
Matching sewing threads*

## THE EMBROIDERY

Cut out the mats and napkins, following the cutting layout shown opposite. The finished fringed edge should be even, so cut straight along the grain.

Following the chart, baste the positioning lines at the bottom right of the fabric, 4cm (1½in) in from both sides. With the fabric stretched in a hoop, complete the embroidery stitching with a single strand of thread. Remove the basting stitches and steam press on the wrong side.

## THE HEM

For the fringed hem, remove a single thread 12mm (½in) in from the outer edge on all four sides. Using matching sewing thread and a round-ended needle, work a single row of hem stitching, taking two threads for each stitch (see page 125). Finally, remove the fabric threads below the hemstitching to complete the fringed edge.

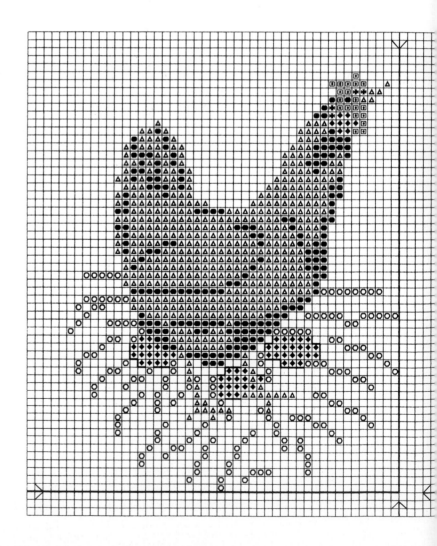

HICKETY, PICKETY ▶

| | |
|---|---|
| ◆ white (bks 453) | ⊡ 3328 red |
| ✱ 977 yellow | △ 413 grey |
| ○ 676 gold | ● 310 black |

## HUMPTY DUMPTY ◀

- ÷ white
- ○ silver thread
- = 743 yellow
- ◣ 741 orange
- △ 434 brown
- ⊡ 839 dark brown
- S 754 flesh
- ◆ 842 fawn
- I 352 pink
- ↓ 351 deep pink
- ◺ 519 blue
- ✱ 517 dark blue
- ● 310 black

CUTTING
LAYOUT

# CORDED CUSHION

This charming cushion,
embroidered in minute detail
and edged with a contrast
twisted cord, is the ideal
accessory for a favourite
armchair or sofa.

### I HAD A LITTLE NUT TREE

I had a little nut tree, nothing would it bear
But a silver nutmeg and a golden pear.
The King of Spain's daughter came to visit me,
And all because of my little nut tree.
I skipped over water, I danced over sea,
And all the birds in the air couldn't catch me.

# TRIM BOOKMARKS

Here are bookmarks to please any reader. Each has a motif delicately edged either with lace and a ribbon rosette or with loop stitch and a fine cotton tassel.

### MARY'S CANARY

Mary had a pretty bird,
Feathers bright and yellow,
Slender legs – upon my word
He was a pretty fellow.

### THE TEN O'CLOCK SCHOLAR

A diller, a dollar, a ten o'clock scholar!
What makes you come so soon?
You used to come at ten o'clock
But now you come at noon.

### MAGPIE, MAGPIE

Magpie, magpie,
Flutter and flee,
Turn up your tail
And good luck come to me.

# TRIM BOOKMARKS

### YOU WILL NEED

For the *Mary's Canary* and *The Ten O'clock Scholar* bookmarks, each measuring about 25cm (10in) long:

*One cream and one white prepared lace-edged bookmark, 18 threads to 2.5cm (1in), each bookmark 5cm (2in) wide (for suppliers, see page 128)*
*DMC stranded embroidery cotton in the colours given in the appropriate panel*
*No26 tapestry needle*

For the *Magpie, Magpie* bookmark, also about 25cm (10in) long:

*23cm (9in) of white evenweave prepared braid, 5cm (2in) wide, 15 threads to 2.5cm (1in)*
*DMC stranded embroidery cotton in the colours given in the appropriate panels*
*No24 tapestry needle*
*Matching sewing thread*

●

### THE EMBROIDERY

Working in an embroidery hoop (see page 121 for the instructions on how to stretch small pieces of fabric in a frame) and with basted centre lines, complete the embroidery, using two strands of thread in the needle throughout.

Remove the basting stitches and, if needed, steam press on the wrong side.

### FINISHING THE MAGPIE BOOKMARK

Make a small double turning on the top edge and, with matching thread, hem in place.

To make a point on the lower edge, fold the bookmark lengthways in half with the wrong side facing out and backstitch the short edges together. Trim the corner, press the seam open and turn to the right side. Flatten out the bookmark, thus creating a point. Press on the wrong side, and slipstitch to hold.

Make the tassel by winding ordinary white

basting thread around a piece of card about 3cm (1¼in) wide. Thread the end into a needle, slip off the tassel threads and bind the loose thread several times around the bunch, close to the top. Pass the needle up through the binding so that it comes out at the top of the tassel — ready to be sewn to the point.

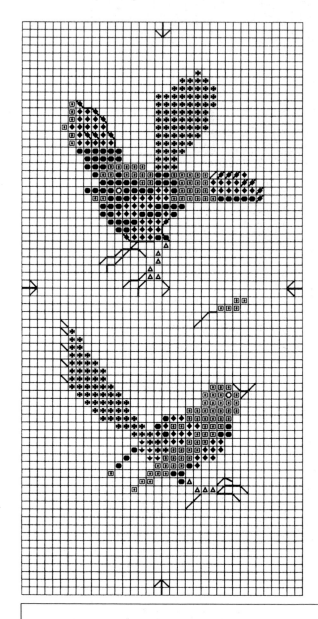

| MAGPIE, MAGPIE ▲ | |
|---|---|
| ◆ white (bks wings 312, body 823) | ☐ 312 blue |
| | ● 823 dark blue |
| ○ 472 gold | △ 3052 olive (bks feet) |
| | ↓ 937 green |
| | ✳ 904 dark green |

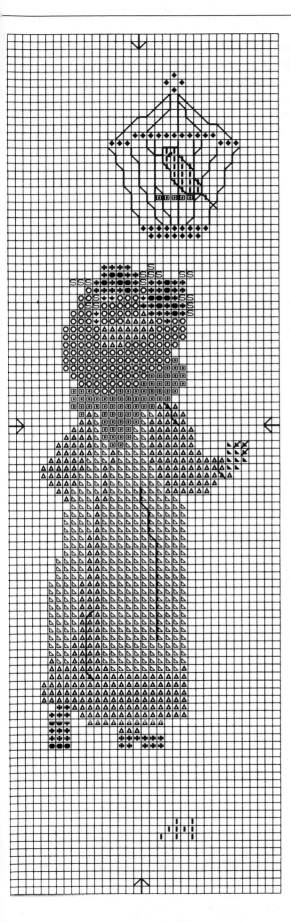

## MARY'S CANARY ◀

- ◣ 948 flesh (bks 3326)
- Ι 445 pale yellow
- ◺ 727 yellow (bks 833)
- ↓ 783 orange
- ○ 833 ochre
- ✳ 3326 pink
- ● 335 deep pink
- △ 794 blue (bks 988)
- ⊟ 913 green
- ◆ 988 dark green
- ⊡ 3011 dark brown

## TEN O'CLOCK SCHOLAR ▶

- ◣ white (and bks 415*)
- Ι 948 flesh
- ✳ 968 pink (bks 3766)
- ○ 3766 sea green (bks 931)
- ● 931 deep blue green
- ◆ 738 straw
- ↓ 435 brown
- △ 612 drab brown
- ⊡ 611 dark brown

*Note: one additional backstitch colour\**

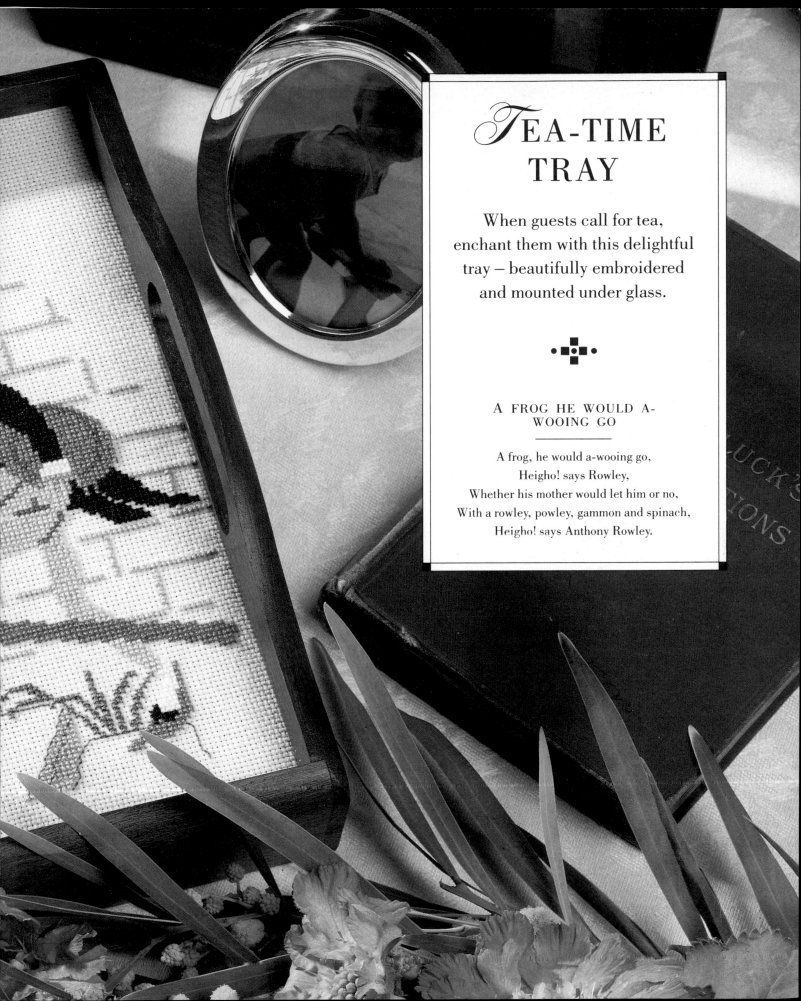

# TEA-TIME TRAY

When guests call for tea, enchant them with this delightful tray – beautifully embroidered and mounted under glass.

### A FROG HE WOULD A-WOOING GO

A frog, he would a-wooing go,
Heigho! says Rowley,
Whether his mother would let him or no,
With a rowley, powley, gammon and spinach,
Heigho! says Anthony Rowley.

## A FROG HE WOULD A-WOOING GO ▲

| | | |
|---|---|---|
| **6** white | **⊟** 3325 pale blue | **△** 830 drab brown |
| **L** 727 yellow | **I** 312 dark blue | **↓** 613 stone (and bks 611*) |
| **◇** gold thread | **A** 734 light olive | **T** 415 pale grey |
| **÷** 676 gold | (and bks 730*) | **=** 414 steel grey (bks 310) |
| **◺** 680 deep gold | **‖** 523 green | **◤** 317 dark grey |
| **H** 754 pale pink | **◆** 367 dark green | **●** 310 black (bks 317) |
| (bks 352) | **↑** 520 dark drab green | *Note: 2 additional* |
| **⊡** 758 pink | **S** 435 light brown | *backstitch colours* |
| **�** 355 red | **○** 832 golden brown | |

# TEA-TIME TRAY

### YOU WILL NEED

For a tray measuring 24cm (9½in) square:

*30cm (12in) square of cream evenweave
Hardanger, 18 threads to 2.5cm (1in)
DMC stranded embroidery cotton in the colours
given in the panel
No26 tapestry needle
Masking tape or strong thread for securing the
mounted fabric
Square wooden tray (for suppliers, see page 128)*

●

### THE EMBROIDERY

With the prepared fabric stretched in an embroidery frame, see page 121, begin the cross stitching, using two strands of thread in the needle. Embroider the main characters first and then the background.

Finish by adding the backstitch details, using a single strand of thread.

Remove the design from the frame and steam press on the wrong side, if necessary.

### ASSEMBLING THE TRAY

Using a soft pencil, mark the supplied mounting card both ways along the centre. This will help you to position the card exactly in the middle of the embroidery. Place the embroidery face down with the card on top and with the pencil lines and basting stitches matching.

Working on one side and then the opposite side, fold over the edges of the fabric on all sides, and secure with one or two pieces of masking tape. When you are sure the design is centred (if not, simply release the masking tape and adjust the fabric until it is correctly positioned), secure the corners firmly.

Turn in each corner to form a mitre (see page 123), and secure with masking tape. Next, finish securing the sides, stretching the fabric evenly, and finally, overcast the mitred corners to finish. Insert the mounted embroidery into the tray, following the manufacturer's instructions.

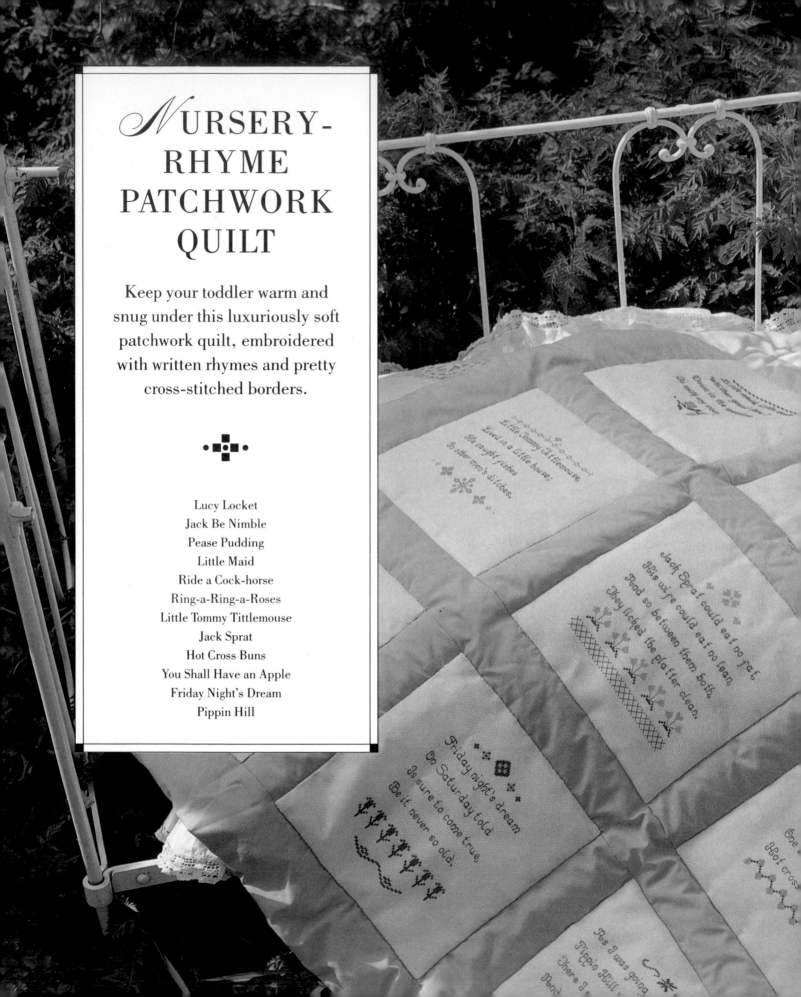

# NURSERY-RHYME PATCHWORK QUILT

Keep your toddler warm and snug under this luxuriously soft patchwork quilt, embroidered with written rhymes and pretty cross-stitched borders.

Lucy Locket
Jack Be Nimble
Pease Pudding
Little Maid
Ride a Cock-horse
Ring-a-Ring-a-Roses
Little Tommy Tittlemouse
Jack Sprat
Hot Cross Buns
You Shall Have an Apple
Friday Night's Dream
Pippin Hill

**TOMMY TITTLEMOUSE** ▲

● 794 pale blue
   791 blue (bks lettering)

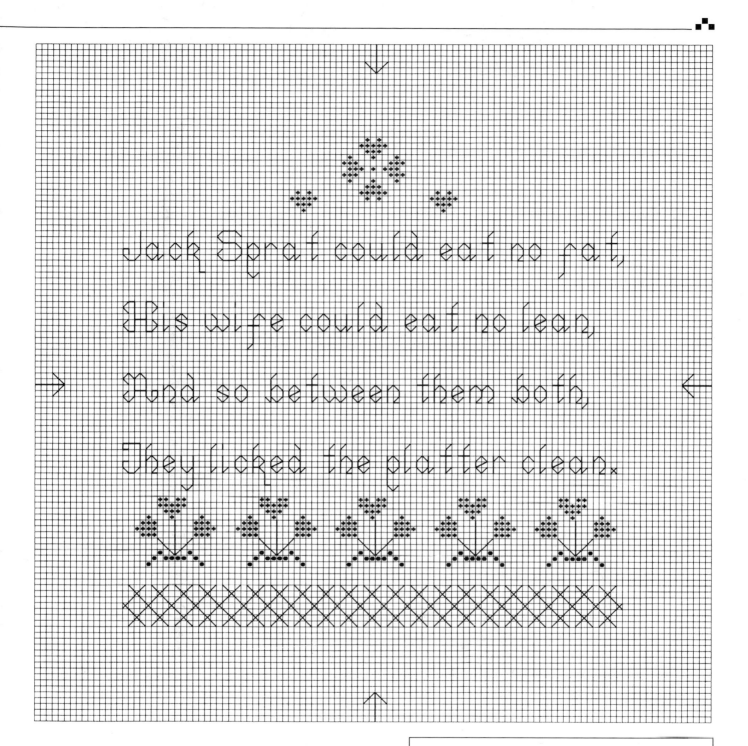

JACK SPRAT ▲

✿ 973 yellow
   321 red (bks lettering)
● 910 green (bks flowers and trellis)

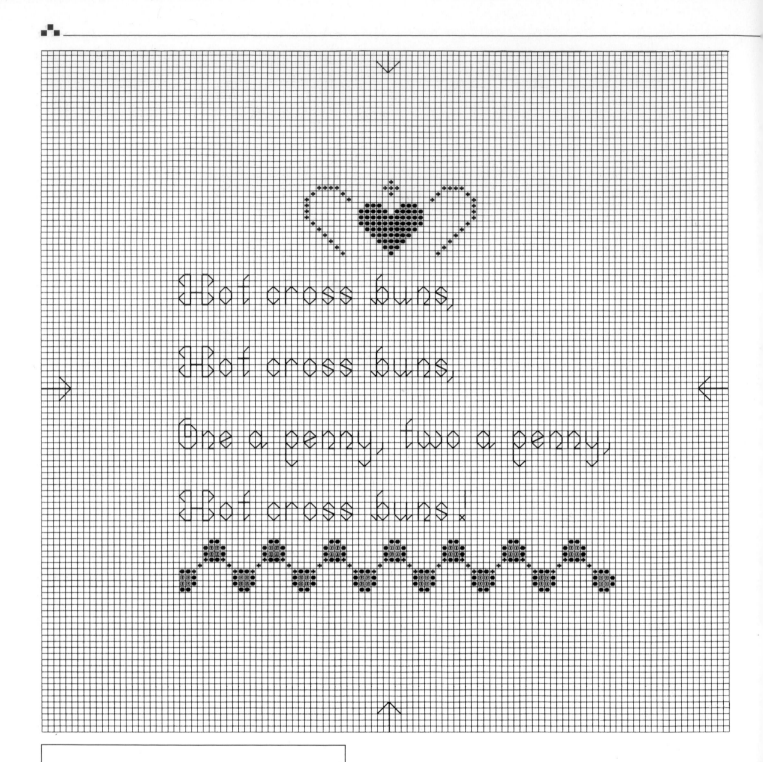

HOT CROSS BUNS ▲

- ▣ 973 yellow
- ● 605 pink
  791 blue (bks lettering)
- ✱ 910 green

You shall have an apple,

You shall have a plum,

You shall have a rattle

When your daddy comes home.

**YOU SHALL HAVE AN APPLE** ▲

- ⊡ 973 yellow
- ● 321 red (bks lettering)
- ✱ 910 green

FRIDAY NIGHT'S DREAM ▲

⊡ 973 yellow
● 321 red
✱ 910 green
   791 blue (bks lettering)

As I was going up Pippin Hill,
Pippin Hill was dirty,
There I met a sweet pretty lass,
And she dropped me a curtsey.

PIPPIN HILL ▲

△ 973 yellow
● 321 red (bks lettering)
✳ 913 pale green
⊡ 910 dark green

# AFTERNOON-TEA CLOTH

Delight your friends with this
perfect party piece — a tablecloth
embroidered with a deep border
of amusing animal motifs,
finished with mitred corners
and hemstitched in the
traditional way.

### THE CAT AND THE FIDDLE

Hey, diddle, diddle!
The cat and the fiddle,
The cow jumped over the moon,
The little dog laughed to see such fun,
And the dish ran away with the spoon.

# AFTERNOON-TEA CLOTH

### YOU WILL NEED

For a tablecloth measuring 102cm (37in) square:

*110cm (43in) of cream evenweave (Aida) fabric,
110cm (43in) wide, 14 threads to 2.5cm (1in); an
8cm (3in) hem allowance is included on all sides
DMC stranded embroidery cotton in the colours
given in the panels; 3 skeins of pale yellow 834
for the hemstitching
No24 tapestry needle
Contrast basting thread*

### PREPARING THE FABRIC

Begin by removing the selvedges from the fabric; check that it is perfectly square and press to remove any creases. Following the positioning diagram on page 58, mark the hem line with basting stitches, measuring 8cm (3in) in on all sides. Mark a second line in the same way, measuring a further 4cm (1½in) in: this is the base line for positioning the motifs. To mark the upright positioning lines, baste a line 11.5cm (4½in) at each side of the centre, on each side. Fold the fabric diagonally both ways; lightly finger press, and baste, as shown in the diagram.

### THE EMBROIDERY

Using an embroidery hoop (see page 121) and following the colour charts given on the previous

**DISH ▶**

- ◆ white (bks 800)
- ○ 951 flesh
  (and bks 3022)*
- △ 800 light blue
- ⊡ 799 blue
- ● 820 royal blue
- ✸ 823 dark blue

pages, complete the embroidery. Use two strands of thread in the needle throughout, with the exception of the eyebrows on the spoon; in this case, use a single strand. Finally, work the backstitching on top.

Following the instructions given on page 123, mitre the corners, and hemstitch the hem, using three strands of pale yellow 834 in the needle. Remove all the basting stitches and steam press the cloth on the wrong side.

THE CAT AND
THE FIDDLE ▶

÷  white (bks on paws
    310)
◻  3047 pale yellow
|  435 ginger (bks 310)
⊡  817 red
△  814 dark red
↑  800 pale blue eyes
=  742 yellow (bks
    eyes 414)
◆  801 brown
↓  938 dark brown
   (bks strings)
◣  414 grey
✷  310 black

*Each of these little vignettes from the tablecloth could be used individually to decorate a tea tray, for example, or perhaps a child's pillowcase. Alternatively, you could make them into pages for a little cloth book.*

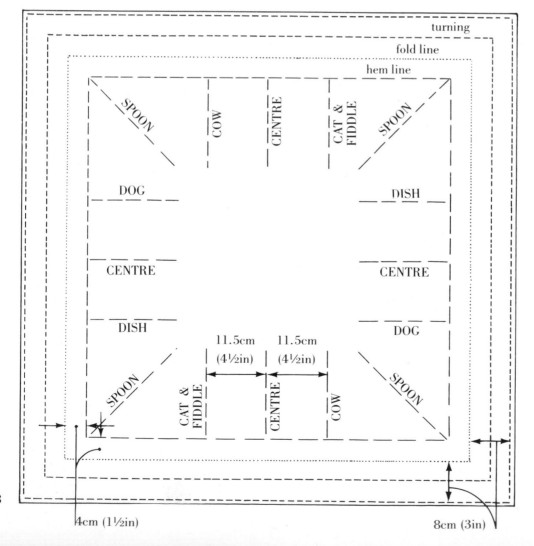

**POSITIONING GUIDE**

turning

fold line

hem line

SPOON

COW

CENTRE

CAT & FIDDLE

SPOON

DOG

DISH

CENTRE

CENTRE

DISH

DOG

SPOON

CAT & FIDDLE

11.5cm (4½in)

11.5cm (4½in)

CENTRE

COW

SPOON

4cm (1½in)

8cm (3in)

**COW ►**

- ○ white (bks cow's back 435, flank 951)
- ↓ 3078 yellow
- ⊡ 951 apricot
- ✳ 3033 beige (bks horns 612, hoofs 801)
- ● 435 brown (and bks 801*)

*Note: one additional backstitch colour**

**DOG ◄**

- ÷ white
- ↑ 3033 flesh
- S 352 pink
- ⊡ 817 red
- △ 814 dark red
- ◣ 833 ochre
- ◆ 434 light brown
- ● 801 dark brown
- ↓ 3011 dark olive brown
- ◺ 415 light grey
- ○ 414 dark grey
- ✳ 310 black (bks 414)

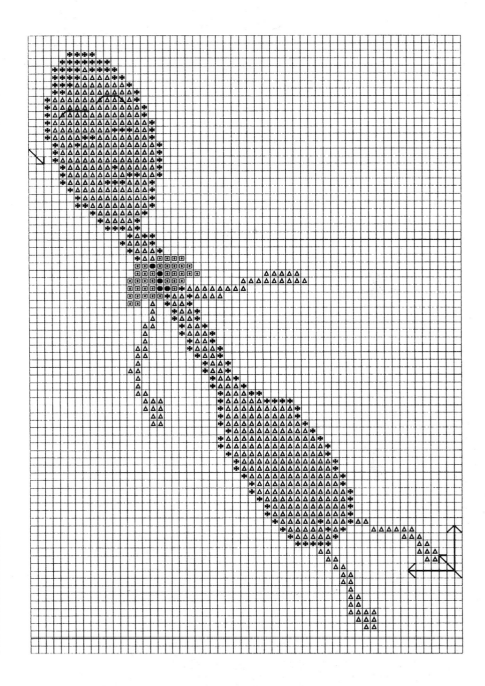

SPOON ▶

⊡ 800 light blue

● 799 blue

△ 762 light grey (bks 414)

✳ 414 dark grey

# BIRTHDAY GREETINGS CARDS

These pleasing little birthday cards will delight any child recipient – and with a little help, children can stitch their own very special greetings.

### THIS LITTLE PIG

This little pig went to market;
This little pig stayed at home;
This little pig had roast beef;
This little pig had none;

•

### A LITTLE MAN

There was a little man, and he
had a little gun,
And his bullets were made of lead, lead, lead.

•

### MISS MUFFET

Little Miss Muffet,
Sat on a tuffet,
Eating her curds and whey;
There came a big spider,
And sat down beside her,
And frightened Miss Muffet away.

## MISS MUFFET ▼

S  744 yellow
◆  948 flesh (bks 352)
⊡  352 pink
✳  210 mauve
↓  3325 pale blue (and bks 322*)
◣  800 blue
Ɩ  3348 green
○  739 beige (and bks 436*)
●  437 light brown (and bks 435*)
△  415 pale grey
*Note: 3 additional
backstitch colours*

## LITTLE PIG ▲

✳  948 flesh (bks 352)
●  352 pink
⊡  800 blue

# BIRTHDAY GREETINGS CARDS

## YOU WILL NEED

For one birthday card, measuring 14cm × 9cm (5½in × 3½in) with a 9cm × 7cm (3½ × 2¾in) oval cut out:

*17cm × 13cm (6¾in × 5in) of white Hardanger fabric, 22 threads to 2.5cm (1in)*
*DMC stranded embroidery cotton in the colours given in the appropriate panel*
*No 26 tapestry needle*
*Birthday card mount (for suppliers, see page 128)*

●

## THE EMBROIDERY

All three cards are stitched in the same way and on the same type of fabric.

Note that it is particularly important with embroidered cards to avoid excessive overstitching on the back, as this would cause unsightly lumps to show through on the right side.

Prepare the fabric and mount it in a small hoop, following the instructions on page 121. Referring to the chart, complete the cross stitching, using a single strand in the needle throughout. Embroider the main areas first and then finish with the backstitching. If necessary, steam press on the wrong side.

It is a good idea to leave the basting stitches in at this stage, as they will prove useful in helping to centre your design in the cut out window.

## MAKING UP THE CARDS

With self-adhesive mounts, this could not be easier! Simply open out the three sections of the card. Trim the embroidery to about 12mm (½in) larger than the marked area around the cut-out window, and then, making sure that the motif is placed in the middle – measure an equal distance at each side of the basting – press it in place. Fold over and press the left-hand section, to cover the design and to give a neat permanent seal.

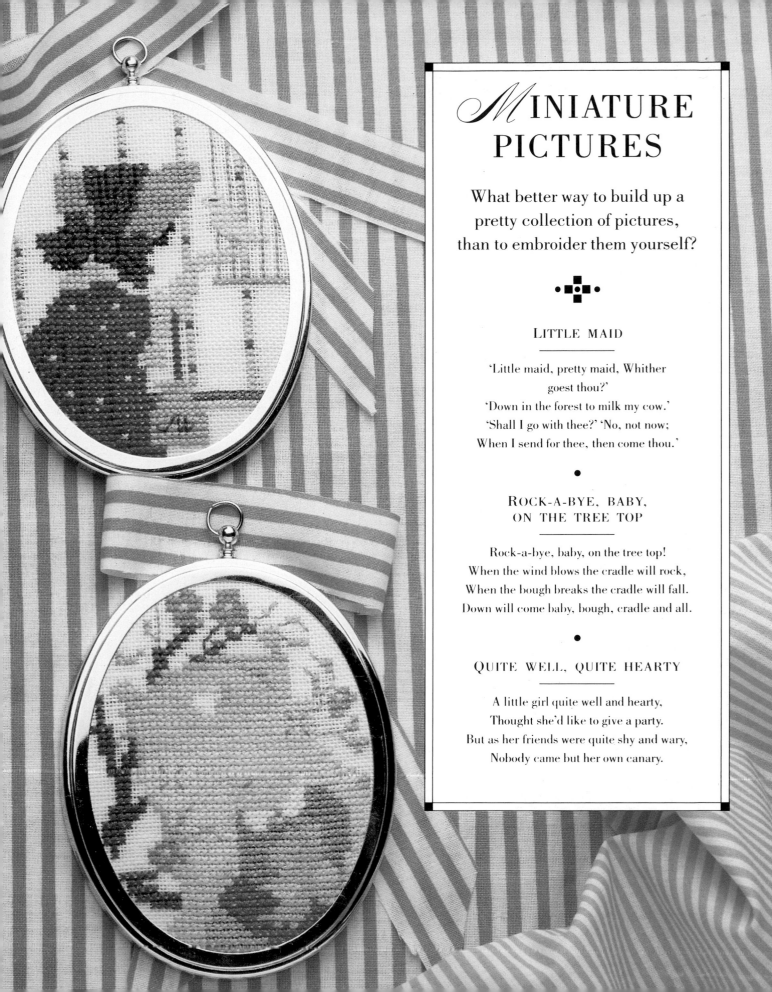

# MINIATURE PICTURES

What better way to build up a
pretty collection of pictures,
than to embroider them yourself?

### LITTLE MAID

'Little maid, pretty maid, Whither
goest thou?'
'Down in the forest to milk my cow.'
'Shall I go with thee?' 'No, not now;
When I send for thee, then come thou.'

### ROCK-A-BYE, BABY,
ON THE TREE TOP

Rock-a-bye, baby, on the tree top!
When the wind blows the cradle will rock,
When the bough breaks the cradle will fall.
Down will come baby, bough, cradle and all.

### QUITE WELL, QUITE HEARTY

A little girl quite well and hearty,
Thought she'd like to give a party.
But as her friends were quite shy and wary,
Nobody came but her own canary.

## QUITE WELL, QUITE HEARTY ▼

- ○ 963 pink (bks 335, initial M 3041)
- ⊡ 335 deep pink (bks 3041)
- ✦ 948 flesh
- ✱ 3041 purple (bks 3011)
- ❙ 966 green
- ◆ 3052 sap green
- ◣ 307 yellow (eye 833)
- △ 833 ochre (bks cage, bird's legs)
- ● 3011 dark brown

## LITTLE MAID ◄

↑ white (and bks 318*)
◣ 948 flesh (bks 352)
○ 352 pink
◺ 800 blue
● 823 navy blue
△ 312 dark blue
⊡ 436 light brown (bks 434)
✜ 434 brown
◆ 415 pale grey
↓ 648 grey
*Note: one additional backstitch colour**

## ROCK-A-BYE BABY ▼

| | |
|---|---|
| = white | ◺ 3756 pale blue |
| ↑ 726 yellow | green (bks 519) |
| I 676 gold | ⊡ 519 blue green |
| ◣ 754 flesh | S 955 pale green |
| (bks eye 3688) | ↓ 913 green (bks twigs) |
| △ 3688 pink | ◆ 951 fawn |
| ● 602 deep pink | ✜ 3011 brown |

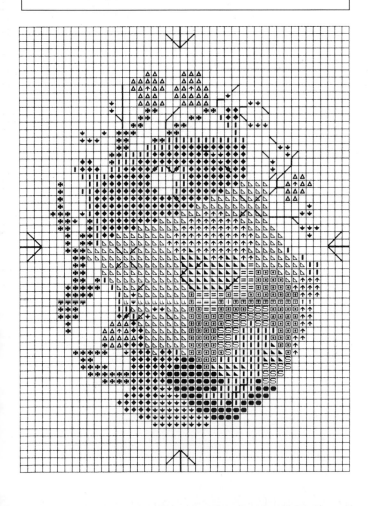

# MINIATURE PICTURES

### YOU WILL NEED

For the *Little Maid* picture, measuring
18cm × 13cm (7¼in × 5in):

*23cm × 18cm (9in × 7¼in) of blue evenweave
(Aida) fabric, 18 threads to 2.5cm (1in)
DMC stranded embroidery cotton in the colours
given in the appropriate panels
No 26 tapestry needle
Oval brass frame (for suppliers, see page 128)*

For *Quite Well, Quite Hearty,* and
*Rock-a-Bye Baby* miniatures, each measuring
11.5cm × 9cm (4½in × 3½in):

*28cm × 18cm (11in × 7¼in) of white evenweave
linen, 26 threads to 2.5 cm (1in)
DMC stranded embroidery cotton in the colours
given in the appropriate panels
No 26 tapestry needle
Two oval brass frames (for suppliers, see page 128)*

•

### THE EMBROIDERY

Each picture is worked in the following way. With
the prepared fabric stretched in a hoop and the
centre marked both ways, see page 121, you are
ready to begin the cross stitching. Use two strands
of thread in the needle throughout, except for the
backstitching of *Little Maid*, which is worked in a
single strand. When working a fairly openweave
fabric, such as the linen used here, bear in mind
that threads should not be stranded across an open
area or they will be seen from the right side.

Remove the fabric from the frame and steam
press on the wrong side, if necessary.

### MAKING UP THE PICTURES

Following the manufacturer's instructions for
assembling the pictures, remembering to check that
you have allowed sufficient fabric to fill the frame
before cutting out (see instructions for assembling
the Dressing-Table Set on page 108).

# PRETTY PINCUSHIONS

Essential for needleworkers!
These pincushions are quick to
make, and roomy enough for a
good supply of pins.

### TWO BIRDS

There were two birds sat on a stone,
Fa, la, la la, lal, de;
One flew away, then there was one,
Fa la, la, la lal, de;

•

### LITTLE MAIDEN

Little maiden, better tarry;
Time enough next year to marry.
Hearts may change, And so may fancy;
Wait a little longer Nancy.

•

### WEE WILLIE WINKIE

Wee Willie Winkie runs through the town;
Upstairs and downstairs, in his nightgown;
Rapping at the window, crying through
the lock,
'Are the children in their beds?
Now it's eight o'clock.'

# PRETTY PINCUSHIONS

## YOU WILL NEED

For the *Two Birds* pincushion, measuring
11.5cm (4½in) across:

*18cm (7¼in) square of cream evenweave
Hardanger, 16 threads to 2.5cm (1in)
DMC stranded embroidery cotton in the colours
given in the appropriate panel
No24 tapestry needle
Pincushion mould with wooden surround
(for suppliers, see page 128)*

For the *Little Maiden* pincushion, measuring
13cm (5in) square:

*Two 15cm (6in) squares of cream evenweave
(Aida) fabric, 14 threads to 2.5cm (1in)
110cm (1⅓yds) of pale pink parcel ribbon
DMC stranded embroidery cotton in the colours
given in the appropriate panel
No24 tapestry needle
Sufficient kapok or sheep's wool for filling
Matching sewing thread*

For *Wee Willie Winkie* pincushion, measuring
13cm (5in) square:

*Two 15cm (6in) squares of grey evenweave
(Aida 705) fabric, 18 threads to 2.5cm (1in)
60cm (24in) of narrow, deep turquoise cord
DMC stranded embroidery cotton in the colours
given in the appropriate panel
No26 tapestry needle
Sufficient kapok or sheep's wool for filling
Matching sewing threads*

•

## THE EMBROIDERY

Work all three pincushions in the following way.
Prepare the fabric and stretch it in a hoop, see page
121, and taking one of the two squares only for the
Little Maiden and Wee Willie Winkie. Complete
the embroidery, using two strands of thread in the
needle. Remove from the frame and steam press on
the wrong side.

## MAKING UP THE PINCUSHIONS

For the *Two Birds* cushion, lay the fabric face down,
with the wooden base centred on top, and draw
around with a soft pencil. Add at least a further
12mm (½in) outside the line and cut out. Run a
gathering thread along the pencil line; centre the
embroidery over the mould, and pin to hold. Pull
up the gathering thread; even out the gathers
around the underside of the mould, and secure the
thread firmly. Attach the mould to the base with the
screw provided.

For the *Little Maiden* and *Wee Willie Winkie*
cushions, in each case place the two sections right
sides together, and then pin and machine stitch
around the edge, taking 12mm (½in) seams and
leaving an 8cm (3in) opening in one side. Turn right
side out and insert the filling. Slipstitch the opening
to close.

For the *Little Maiden*, cut the ribbon into four
equal lengths and tie a bow around each corner,
taking the ribbon twice around before tying. For
*Wee Willie Winkie*, slipstitch the cord around the
edge (see page 124), looping the cord into a circle
approximately 12mm (½in) in diameter at each
corner, as shown in the photograph.

## TWO BIRDS ▼

◁ white

◀ 444 yellow

△ 3733 pale pink

⊡ 893 deep pink

○ 3761 pale pink

✱ 334 blue (bks bird's feet, small bird's head and body)

● 322 dark blue (bks eye, small bird's wings)

� 471 green (bks tree and ground)

↓ 912 veridian green

I 3756 pale grey

## WEE WILLIE WINKIE ▲

◆ 444 yellow

↓ 680 ochre

○ 948 flesh (and bks 224*)

● 899 pink

⊡ 3761 pale blue (bks 807)

I 807 blue

△ 644 stone

✱ 413 dark grey (and bks 318*)

*Note: 2 additional backstitch colours**

## LITTLE MAIDEN ◀

↑ white (bks bloomers and collar 471, bks boy's shirt 799)

I 834 straw

⊐ 948 flesh

◀ 605 pale pink

⊡ 3731 pink

● 602 deep pink

✱ 892 red

○ 3766 light blue

△ 799 blue

◁ 3348 bright green

◆ 471 green

↓ 3011 brown

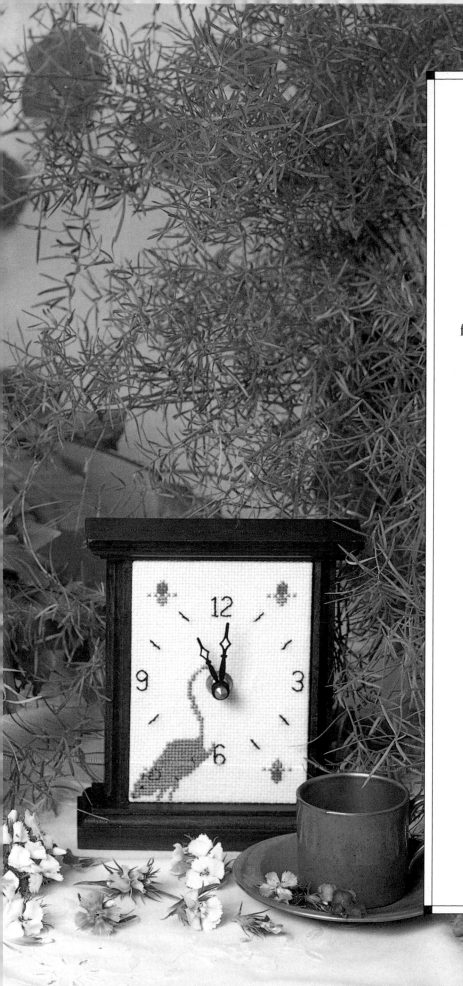

# COFFEE TIME COMPANIONS

Pretty and practical! Keep your coffee piping hot and your table top protected with this snugly-fitting cosy and coffee-pot stand, and so that you don't miss your coffee break, keep the carriage clock to hand.

### POLLY PUT THE KETTLE ON

Polly, put the kettle on,
Polly, put the kettle on,
Polly, put the kettle on,
We'll all have tea.

•

### COFFEE AND TEA

Molly, my sister and I fell out,
And what do you think it was all about?
She loved coffee and I loved tea,
And that was the reason we couldn't agree.

•

### HICKORY, DICKORY, DOCK

Hickory, dickory, dock!
The mouse ran up the clock;
The clock struck one,
And down he ran,
Hickory, dickory, dock.

COFFEE AND TEA ▲
●

I  white (bks 927)            ◆ 3756 pale blue

◣ 834 gold (bks 642)          △ 927 blue green

○ 3774 flesh (bks 224)        ⊡ 926 deep blue green

● 224 dusky pink              ↓ 642 coffee (bks 371)

                              ✺ 371 brown (bks kettle handle)

# COFFEE-POT STAND

### YOU WILL NEED

A hexagonal stand measuring 18cm (7in) with
a 13cm (5in) circular centre:

*20cm (8in) square of cream Hardanger fabric,
18 threads to 2.5cm (1in)
DMC stranded embroidery cotton in the colours
given in the panel
No26 tapestry needle
coffee pot stand (for suppliers, see page 128)*

### THE EMBROIDERY

Working in a hoop with the centre lines basted both
ways, see page 121, begin the embroidery. Following the chart given opposite, use two strands of
thread in the needle for the cross stitching and a
single strand for the backstitching. Leaving the
basting stitches in place, steam press the finished
embroidery on the wrong side.

### ASSEMBLING THE STAND

To get an exact fit, cut out the embroidery,
following the instructions given for The Traditional
Dressing-Table Set on page 108. After that,
assemble the stand according to the manufac-
urer's instructions.

# CARRIAGE CLOCK

## YOU WILL NEED

For clock measuring overall 16.5cm × 13cm
(6½in × 5in) with a 13cm × 9cm
(5in × 3½in) face:

*20cm × 16.5cm (8in × 6½in) of cream*
*Hardanger fabric, 16 threads to 2.5cm (1in)*
*DMC stranded embroidery cotton in the colours*
*given in the panel*
*No24 tapestry needle*
*Carriage clock (for suppliers, see page 128)*
*Strong thread for mounting the embroidery*

*Alternative suggestions for the clock face numerals.*

## THE EMBROIDERY

It should be possible to stitch such a small amount of embroidery in the hand without running the risk of distorting the fabric. Whichever way you choose to work, mark the centre both ways with basting stitches. Note that the centre of the clock face is higher than the centre of the embroidery, and should also be marked with a pencil.

Using two strands of thread in the needle throughout, follow the chart and complete the embroidery. When stitching the numerals, remember to start and finish with each one; do not strand from one to another or this will show on the right side. Steam press the finished embroidery on the wrong side.

## ASSEMBLING THE CLOCK

Follow the manufacturer's instructions for mounting the embroidery and assembling the clock. See also Basic Skills, page 124, for lacing and mounting an embroidery.

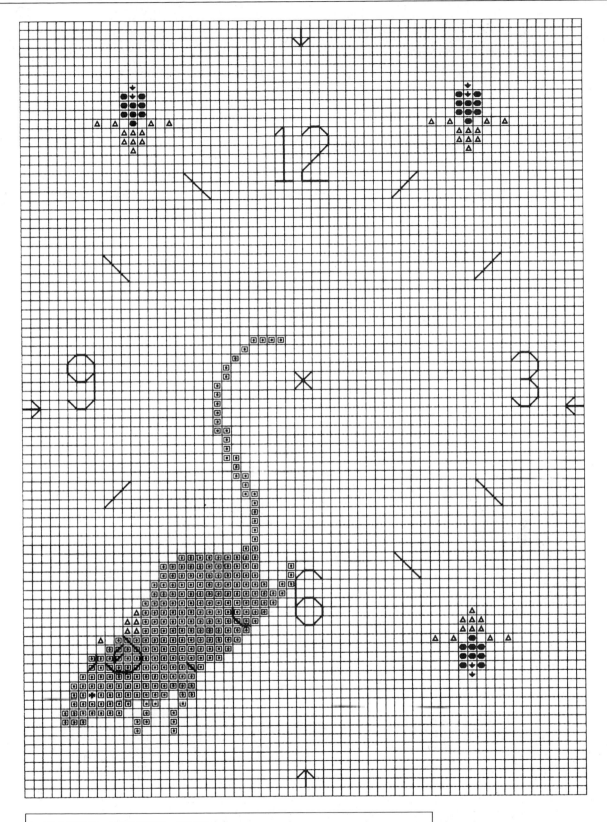

HICKORY, DICKORY, DOCK ▲

↓ 832 yellow          △ 472 green          ✿ 310 black

● 3731 pink          ⊡ 3023 fawn (bks 610)          (bks numerals)

# CHRISTMAS GREETINGS CARDS

What better way to personalize your greetings than to embroider them yourself? Using prepared mounts, you can give them a truly professional finish.

### LITTLE JACK HORNER

Little Jack Horner sat in a corner,
Eating a Christmas pie;
He put in his thumb, and pulled out a plum,
And said, 'What a good boy am I!'

### DAME GET UP

Dame, get up and bake your pies,
Bake your pies, bake your pies,
Dame get up and bake your pies
On Christmas day in the morning.

### I SAW THREE SHIPS

I saw three ships come sailing by,
Come sailing by, come sailing by,
I saw three ships come sailing by,
On New Year's day in the morning.

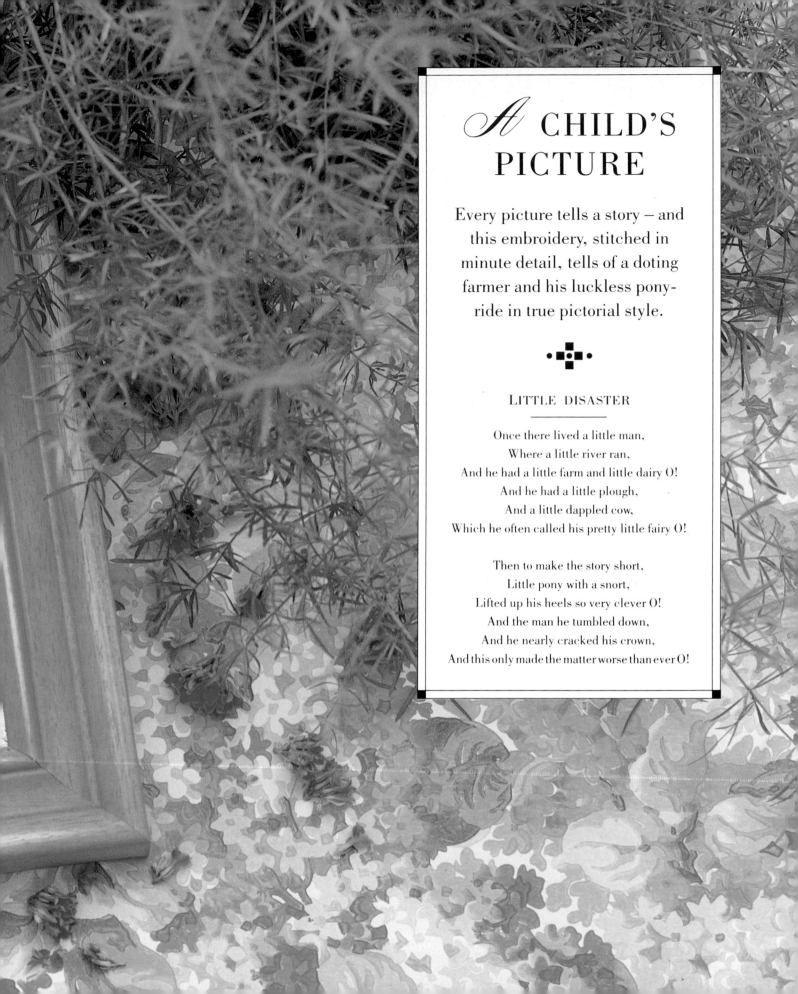

# *A* CHILD'S PICTURE

Every picture tells a story – and this embroidery, stitched in minute detail, tells of a doting farmer and his luckless pony-ride in true pictorial style.

❖

### LITTLE DISASTER

Once there lived a little man,
Where a little river ran,
And he had a little farm and little dairy O!
And he had a little plough,
And a little dappled cow,
Which he often called his pretty little fairy O!

Then to make the story short,
Little pony with a snort,
Lifted up his heels so very clever O!
And the man he tumbled down,
And he nearly cracked his crown,
And this only made the matter worse than ever O!

## LITTLE DISASTER ▶

- T white
- H 745 pale yellow (and bks 742*)
- S 677 pale gold (and bks 729*)
- ÷ 722 orange
- △ 783 ochre
- ● 951 flesh (and bks 758*)
- | 435 rust (and bks 300*)
- ◇ 519 blue
- ↑ 472 pale green
- ◺ 469 sap green (and bks 935*)
- ↓ 503 blue green (and bks 500*)
- || 3345 dark green
- × 712 cream (and bks 842*)
- ◣ 822 beige (bks 640)
- ✱ 3045 light brown (bks 435)
-   839 dark brown (bks 435)
- ◆ 3072 pale grey
- ○ 926 blue grey (and bks 311*)
- ● 310 black (bks 712)

*Note: 8 additional backstitch colours**

# A CHILD'S PICTURE

## YOU WILL NEED

For an unframed picture measuring
23cm (9in) square:

*35cm (14in) square of blue evenweave (Aida)
fabric, 18 threads to 2.5cm (1in)
23cm (9in) square of lightweight batting
DMC stranded embroidery cotton in the colours
given in the panel
No26 tapestry needle
23cm (9in) square of 3mm (⅛in) cardboard
Masking tape for securing the mounted fabric
Picture frame of your choice*

•

## THE EMBROIDERY

Referring to the instructions on page 121, stretch the prepared fabric in a frame. Using two strands of thread in the needle and carefully following the chart, begin the embroidery. Work the outline and the two horizontal dividing lines first, making sure you count the correct number of threads between.

Finish the cross stitching and, using a single strand of thread, work the backstitching to complete the embroidery.

Remove the embroidery from the frame and, if necessary, steam press on the wrong side.

## FRAMING THE PICTURE

To offset the embroidery, the picture here includes a border of background fabric 2cm (¾in) wide, which you can easily adjust to suit your own preference. You may wish, for example, to add a decorative outer border in cross stitching, choosing one of the borders given at the end of the book. Also, to give the finished picture a slightly padded look, a layer of lightweight batting is inserted between the fabric and mounting card.

Mount the picture, following the instructions given for the Tea-time Tray on page 36, before finally inserting it into the picture frame.

# BORDERED PICTURES

Transform a simple illustration into an appealing picture by framing it with a border of motifs taken from the design itself.

### JACK AND JILL

Jack and Jill went up the hill
To fetch a pail of water;
Jack fell down and broke his crown
And Jill came tumbling after.

•

### TOMMY TITTLEMOUSE

Little Tommy Tittlemouse
Lived in a little house;
He caught fishes
In other men's ditches.

•

### TOM, TOM, THE PIPER'S SON

Tom, Tom, the piper's son,
Stole a pig and away he ran.
The pig was eat and Tom was beat,
And Tom went crying down the street.

# BORDERED PICTURES

## YOU WILL NEED

For the *Jack and Jill* picture, measuring
23cm × 16.5cm (9in × 6½in):

*30cm × 24cm (12in × 9½in) of cream evenweave
(Aida) fabric, 14 threads to 2.5 cm (1in)
DMC stranded embroidery cotton in the colours
given in the panel on page 93
No24 tapestry needle
24cm × 18cm (9½in × 7¼in) of 3mm (⅛in)
cardboard for mounting the embroidery
24cm × 18cm (9½in × 7¼in) of lightweight
synthetic batting
Masking tape or strong thread for securing the
mounted fabric
Picture frame of your choice*

For the *Tommy Tittlemouse* picture, measuring
16.5cm × 14cm (6½in × 5½in):

*23cm × 25cm (9in × 10in) of white evenweave
(Aida) fabric, 14 threads to 2.5 cm (1in)
DMC stranded embroidery cotton in the colours
given in the panel on this page
No24 tapestry needle
18cm × 15cm (7¼in × 6in) of 3mm (⅛in)
cardboard for mounting the embroidery
18cm × 15cm (7¼in × 6in) of lightweight
synthetic batting
Masking tape or strong thread and picture frame,
see above*

For *Tom, Tom, the Piper's Son* picture, measuring
20cm × 16.5cm (8in × 6½in):

*23cm × 24cm (9in × 9½in) of blue evenweave
(Aida) fabric, 14 threads to 2.5 cm (1in)
DMC stranded embroidery cotton in the colours
given in the panel on page 94
No24 tapestry needle
21.5cm × 18cm (8½in × 7¼in) of 3mm (⅛in)
cardboard for mounting the embroidery
21.5cm × 18cm (8½in × 7¼in) of lightweight
synthetic batting
Masking tape or strong thread and picture frame,
see above*

## THE EMBROIDERY

The embroidery for all three pictures is worked in
the same way.

Begin by preparing the edges of the fabric and
stretching it in an embroidery frame. Next, baste
the centre lines in both directions, following the
instructions given on page 121.

Working with two strands of thread in the
needle throughout, complete the cross stitching,
referring to the appropriate chart and colour key.
Finish embroidering the main characters before
working the background and, finally, stitching
the border.

Remove the fabric from the frame and, if necessary, steam press on the wrong side. Do not take
out the basting stitches at this stage – they will
be used as a guide when centring the mounting
card on the fabric.

TOMMY TITTLEMOUSE ◀

↑ white (bks 642)
● yellow (bks 732)
○ 741 orange
↓ 832 ochre
◣ 948 flesh (bks eye 732)
◆ 224 pink
⊡ 3328 red
÷ 598 blue
 (bks water, clouds)

✱ 732 olive (bks birds
 and fishing line;
 bks 832)
= 3348 light green
I 913 green
◣ 943 dark green
S 642 fawn (bks 535)
△ 640 brown
● 535 dark grey

JACK AND JILL ▲

● white (bks 827)
◺ 729 yellow
÷ 3046 corn (bks 3072)
↑ 950 flesh (bks 224)
△ 224 pink (bks 611)
● 3731 deep pink
= 827 pale blue (bks 3052)
○ 799 blue
↓ 772 light green
◆ 3052 sage green (bks 829)
⊡ 611 brown (bks 829)
✱ 829 dark brown (bks bucket)
◣ 3072 grey (and bks 453*)
I 472 green
*Note: one additional
backstitch colour**

## MAKING UP THE PICTURES

To facilitate framing, an extra 12mm (½in) has been allowed each way, but the size of the cardboard can easily be adjusted to suit the measurements of a particular frame. You may prefer to add a much wider border of fabric around the embroidery before mounting and framing. In this case, remember to allow for the additional measurement to the ground fabric, and mounting board, before you begin the embroidery.

The pictures here have also been given a slightly padded look by inserting a layer of batting between the embroidery and the cardboard mount.

Make up the pictures in the same way as the Tea-time Tray on page 36, but before you attach the fabric to the back of the card, draw around the edges of the card with pencil. Remove the card, place the batting in position on the embroidery, and then replace the card on top and continue as before.

Finally, insert the finished picture into your frame. A simple alternative to traditional framing is to display your embroidery in a glass frame. Here, the fabric is placed between two pieces of glass, which are clipped around the edges.

**TOM, TOM, THE PIPER'S SON** ▶

| | white
S | 948 flesh (bks 352)
✦ | 754 pale pink
△ | 352 pink
◣ | 977 orange
↑ | 834 ochre
⊡ | 436 brown
● | 869 dark brown
○ | 800 blue
◆ | 503 green
◿ | 502 mid-green
✳ | 500 dark green

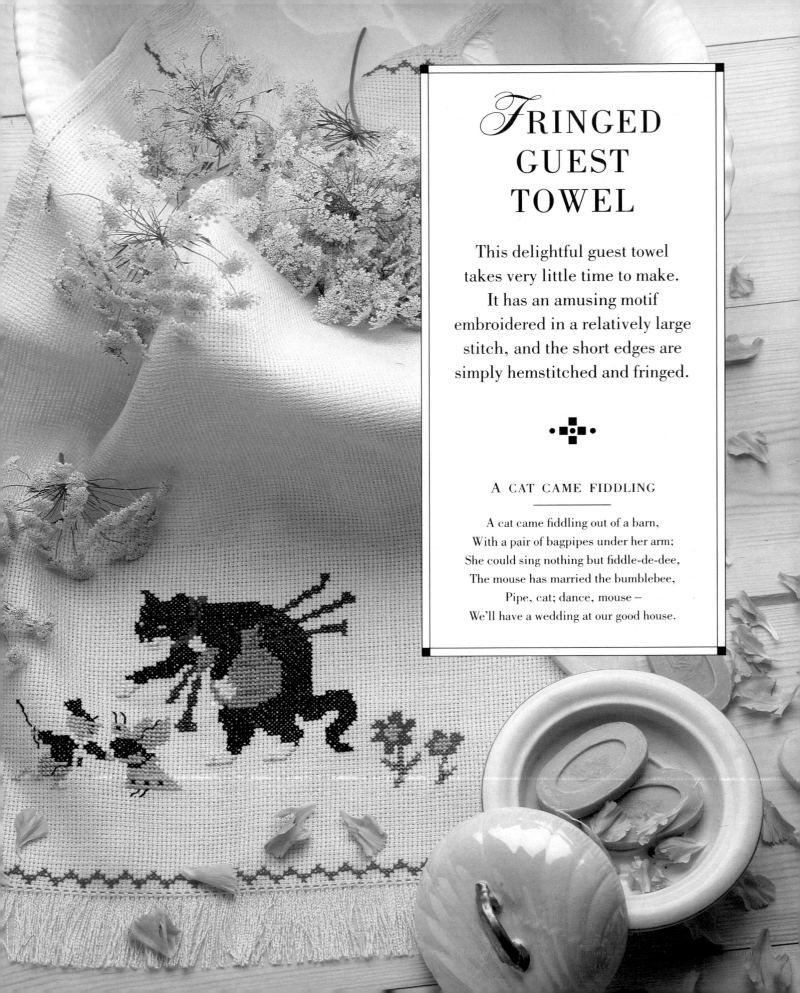

# FRINGED GUEST TOWEL

This delightful guest towel
takes very little time to make.
It has an amusing motif
embroidered in a relatively large
stitch, and the short edges are
simply hemstitched and fringed.

### A CAT CAME FIDDLING

A cat came fiddling out of a barn,
With a pair of bagpipes under her arm;
She could sing nothing but fiddle-de-dee,
The mouse has married the bumblebee,
Pipe, cat; dance, mouse –
We'll have a wedding at our good house.

A CAT CAME FIDDLING ▲

| | |
|---|---|
| = white (bks 927) | ⌐ 869 brown |
| ÷ 725 yellow | △ 801 dark brown |
| ◣ 729 ochre | ◸ 778 pink |
| | ✱ 304 red |

| |
|---|
| ◆ 3705 vermilian red |
| ● 902 dark red |
| ↑ 472 light green |
| ↓ 3347 green |

$\square$ 927 pale grey (bks 413)
$\boxdot$ 413 dark grey
$\bigcirc$ 310 black (bks hat brim, walking stick, bee's
    antennae and feet)

# FRINGED
# GUEST TOWEL

## YOU WILL NEED

For a guest towel measuring 69cm × 42cm
(27in × 16½in):

*69cm × 47cm (27in × 18½in) of cream or white
huckaback, 10 stitches to 2.5cm (1in); any suitable
soft fabric, such as Zweigart's Tula, can be used
DMC stranded embroidery cotton in the colours
given in the panel, plus one skein of ecru
for the hemstitching
No18 tapestry needle
Matching sewing thread*

•

## THE EMBROIDERY

*Hems* Hemstitch the finished edges of the guest
towel before completing the cross stitch motif in a
hoop.

For the fringed edges, follow the instructions
given on page 125 and work a single row of hemstitching across the two short edges, placing the
stitching line 4cm (1½in) in from the raw edge; first
making sure the raw edge is cut straight along the
grain. Using three strands of matching stranded
cotton in the needle, work over two squares across
and one square deep for each stitch.

On the two long edges, first baste a 12mm (½in)
double turning. With the right side facing, hemstitch to hold the hem in place. Work the hemstitching as before, but make sure when passing the
needle behind that it enters the fabric at right
angles – not only to secure the hem but to give a
neat appearance to the stitches on the wrong side.

*Motif* Baste the positioning lines for the embroidered motif, following the chart given opposite, and
then, referring to the colour key, complete the cross
stitching.

If needed, steam press on the wrong side. Finish
by removing the threads below the hemstitching to
complete the fringed edges.

# VICTORIAN-STYLE FOOTSTOOL

The enduring charm of heraldic
design – adapted here on this
traditional rosewood footstool
– is sure to make it a
family favourite.

### THE LION AND THE UNICORN

The lion and the unicorn were fighting for
the crown,
The lion beat the unicorn all around the town.
Some gave them white bread, and some gave
them brown,
Some gave them plum-cake and sent them
out of town.

# VICTORIAN-STYLE
# FOOTSTOOL

## YOU WILL NEED

For a footstool measuring 30cm (12in) across:

*46cm (18in) square of grey evenweave (Aida 718)
fabric, 14 threads to 2.5cm (1in)
DMC stranded embroidery cotton in the colours
given in the panel
No24 tapestry needle
Round footstool with wooden surround
(for suppliers, see page 128)*

•

## THE EMBROIDERY

Prepare the fabric and stretch it in an embroidery frame, following the instructions given on page 121.

The cross stitching is worked with two strands of thread in the needle, with the exception of the unicorn. This is worked in three strands to emphasize the colour. Begin the cross stitching, working outwards from the middle, leaving the white unicorn until last.

Remove the finished embroidery from the frame, and if necessary, steam press it on the wrong side.

## MAKING UP THE FOOTSTOOL

Follow the manufacturer's instructions for assembling the footstool, but first make a preliminary check to see if, with the top fabric (the embroidery) included, the mould fits snugly inside the outer wooden frame. If not, then it is a good idea to add a layer of synthetic batting underneath the top fabric.

Complete the assembly, but before using the footstool, coat the embroidered surface with a proprietry dust-repellant spray, as recommended by upholsterers.

THE LION AND THE
UNICORN ◄

⊖ white (bks 928)

◣ 822 cream

÷ 725 yellow (bks 831)

= 676 corn (bks on white bread)

○ 734 gold (bks 831)

◆ 831 ochre

● 3712 red

△ 598 blue

◺ 3348 light green

S 989 green

⊡ 992 veridian green

↓ 320 dark green

✳ 3045 brown (bks on brown
    bread)

928 grey

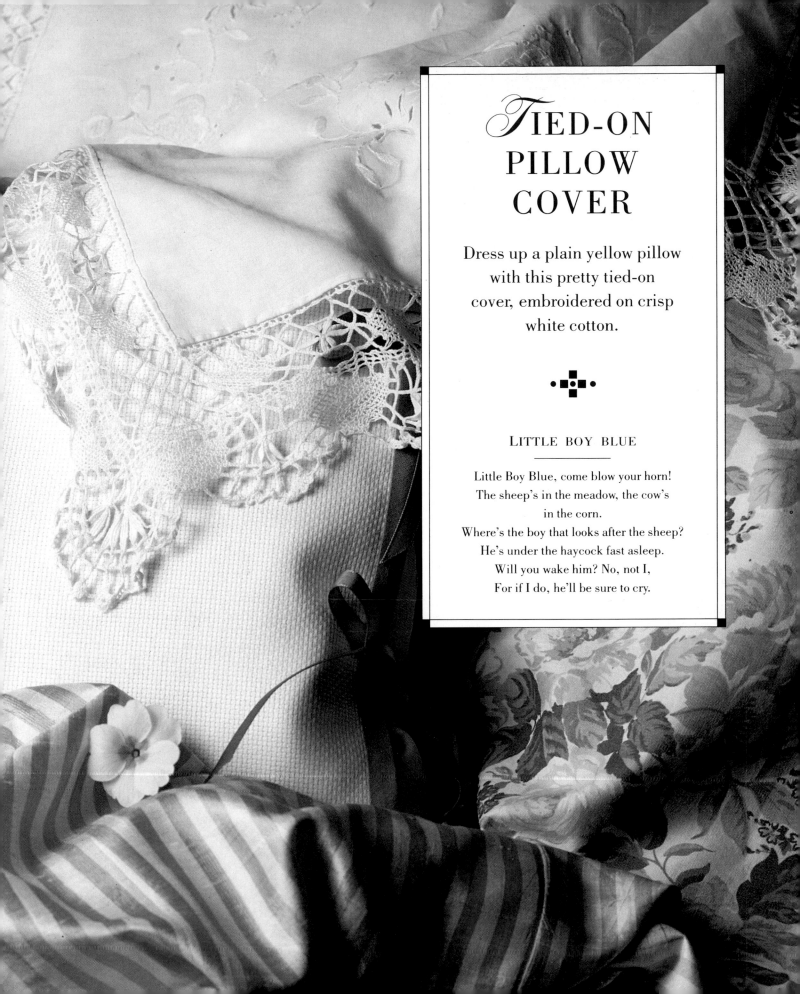

# TIED-ON PILLOW COVER

Dress up a plain yellow pillow with this pretty tied-on cover, embroidered on crisp white cotton.

❖

### LITTLE BOY BLUE

Little Boy Blue, come blow your horn!
The sheep's in the meadow, the cow's
in the corn.
Where's the boy that looks after the sheep?
He's under the haycock fast asleep.
Will you wake him? No, not I,
For if I do, he'll be sure to cry.

# TIED-ON PILLOW COVER

### YOU WILL NEED

For a pillow cover measuring 46cm × 35cm
(18in × 14in):

*48.5cm × 38cm (19in × 15in) of white evenweave
(Aida) fabric, 14 threads to 2.5cm (1in)*
*48.5cm × 38cm (19in × 15in) of white backing
fabric, either fine cotton or linen*
*250cm (2⅔yds) of cornflower blue satin ribbon,
2cm (¾in) wide*
*140cm (1½yds) of cornflower blue bias binding*
*DMC stranded embroidery cotton in the colours
given in the panel*
*No24 tapestry needle*
*Matching sewing thread*

•

### THE EMBROIDERY

With the prepared fabric stretched in a frame, see
page 121, baste the positioning lines for the motif
at the bottom left of the fabric, 12cm (4¾in) in from
both sides, following the chart opposite.

Using two strands of thread in the needle
throughout, work all the cross stitching first and
then the backstitching.

Take out the basting stitches; remove the fabric
from the frame, and steam press on the wrong side.

### MAKING UP THE PILLOW COVER

With right sides together, baste the top
and backing fabric along the two long edges.
Machine stitch, taking 12mm (½in) seams. Press
the seams open.

For the ties, cut the ribbon into eight equal
lengths. With the wrong side facing, baste them
in pairs to each of the short edges, placing
them 10cm (4in) in from the corners (see the
diagram below).

Cover the short edges with bias binding, at the
same time enclosing the ribbon ends. Overlap the
raw edges of the binding at the seams. Press and
turn through to the right side. Slip the cover over
a contrast pillow and tie in place.

---

LITTLE BOY BLUE ▶

◺ white (bks 341)
◢ 744 yellow (bks 738)
↓ 738 corn
◆ 834 deep yellow
| 3779 flesh (bks 3712)
△ 3712 red (bks 3052)
○ 341 blue (bks 792)
● 792 dark blue (bks eye;
    bks 3011)
✱ 3052 olive
⊡ 3011 brown

---

# TRADITIONAL DRESSING-TABLE SET

Embroider these delightful
dressing-table accessories,
choosing – if you like – an
alternative background colour to
suit your bedroom decor.

### CURLY-LOCKS

Curly-locks, Curly-locks, wilt thou be mine?
Thou shalt not wash the dishes, nor yet
feed the swine;
But sit upon a cushion, and sew a fine seam,
And feed upon strawberries, sugar and cream.

### SLEEP BABY, SLEEP

Sleep, baby, sleep,
Our cottage vale is deep:
The little lamb is on the green,
With woolly fleece so soft and clean –
Sleep, baby, sleep.

### TWINKLE, TWINKLE, LITTLE STAR

Twinkle, twinkle, little star,
How I wonder what you are!
Up above the sky so high,
Like a diamond in the sky.

# TRADITIONAL DRESSING-TABLE SET

### YOU WILL NEED

For the dressing-table set – handmirror with back measuring 13cm × 11.5cm (5in × 4½in), hairbrush with back measuring 10cm × 9cm (4in × 3½in), trinket box with lid measuring 10cm (4in) across:

*45cm × 20cm (18in × 8in) of blue evenweave fabric (Aida 503), 18 threads to 2.5cm (1in)*
*DMC stranded embroidery cotton in the colours given in the panels*
*No26 tapestry needle*
*Dressing-table set, plus trinket box*
*(for suppliers, see page 128)*

•

### THE EMBROIDERY

As an alternative to setting individual pieces of fabric in a small embroidery hoop, you may find it easier and more economical to work all three designs on one piece of fabric, stretched in a rectangular frame. In either case, use basting stitches to divide the area into three equal sections measuring 20cm × 15cm (8in × 6in).

Baste the central positioning lines on each section, ready for cross stitching the motifs. Referring to the charts, complete the embroidery; use two strands of thread throughout, with the exception of the stars on the trinket box, which are worked in a single strand. To make the stars, see Eyelet Stitch on page 125. Remove the finished embroidery from the frame and, if necessary, steam press on the wrong side.

### ASSEMBLING THE DRESSING-TABLE SET

The paper templates supplied by the manufacturers may vary in size so, in order to get an exact fit for each piece, cut out the embroidery, using the template supplied with each piece, but first mark the centre on the template both ways in pencil. In each case, place the template with the marked side on the wrong side of the embroidery; match the pencil

lines to the basting stitches, and draw around with a soft pencil. This will help you to centre your embroidery. Before cutting out, place the template inside the particular frame and check to see how much more fabric, if any, should be included beyond the pencil line. This is a critical stage in the assembly, because the return on the frames is very shallow and therefore does not allow for the fabric to be cut too small. Cut out the fabric and remove the basting stitches.

Complete the assembly of all three pieces, following the manufacturer's instructions.

### SLEEP BABY, SLEEP ▲

| | | | |
|---|---|---|---|
| ◺ | white | ◤ | 800 blue |
| ⊊ | 834 yellow (and stars) | ● | 798 dark blue |
| △ | 3045 ochre | I | 3347 green |
| ○ | 754 flesh (bks eye 3045) | | (bks 3052) |
| ✿ | 3354 pink | ◆ | 3072 grey (bks legs 798) |
| ⊡ | 3328 red (and bks 3052 *) | | *Note: one additional backstitch colour** |

### CURLY-LOCKS ◀

◹ white (bks 452)

⊡ 452 stone

S 3078 yellow (bks 734)

◆ 734 ochre (bks 3052)

◤ 754 flesh (bks 224)

✦ 224 pink

✹ 352 deep pink (bks
  embroidery thread)

● 798 blue

○ 3053 green

△ 3052 sage

### TWINKLE, TWINKLE ▶

◆ white (and bks 793*)

○ 3078 lemon (and eyelet stitch stars)

⊡ 676 yellow

✦ 754 flesh (bks 3354)

✹ 3354 pink (and bks eye)

● 899 red (bks 793)

*Note: one additional backstitch
colour*; stitch the eye as shown below:*

| 793 blue (one upright bks eye)

# Lace-edged Cushions

Pretty and feminine, these lace-edged cushions — made singly or as a pair — will add a touch of luxury and comfort to a young girl's room.

### RIDE A COCK-HORSE

Ride a cock-horse to Banbury Cross
To see a fine lady upon a white horse.
With rings on her fingers
And bells on her toes,
She shall have music wherever she goes.

•

### LITTLE BO-PEEP

Little Bo-Peep has lost her sheep
And doesn't know where to find them.
Leave them alone,
And they will come home
Wagging their tails behind them.

RIDE A COCK HORSE ▲  ○ 743 yellow (bks on saddle  ∽ 676 gold      ◆ 554 lilac (and bks 550*)
  ‖ white (bks 414)            blanket)              ÷ 948 flesh (bks 352)  Ⅰ 800 blue
  ⊖ 745 pale yellow (bks 436)  △ gold thread (bks 839)  ⊡ 352 pink       ↓ 436 light brown (and bks 433*

# RIDE A COCK-HORSE

## YOU WILL NEED

For a cover measuring 35cm (14in) square:

*40cm (16in) square of blue evenweave (Aida)
fabric, 14 threads to 2.5cm (1in)
38cm (15in) square of blue floral print backing
fabric; 12mm (½in) seam allowances are included
150cm (1⅔yds) of white pre-gathered lace trim,
4cm (1½in) wide
DMC stranded embroidery cotton in the colours
given in the panel
No 24 tapestry needle
Matching sewing thread
38cm (15in) square cushion pad*

•

## THE EMBROIDERY

Following the instructions given on page 121, prepare and stretch your fabric in an embroidery frame. Using two strands of thread in the needle throughout, complete the cross stitching. Work the backstitching on top, using a single strand of thread. Remove the embroidery from the frame, and steam press on the wrong side.

## MAKING UP THE CUSHION

Before removing the basting threads, trim the embroidery to measure 38cm (15in) square, using the threads as a guide for measuring and thus keeping the design in the centre of the fabric.

Using a tiny french seam, join the raw edges of the lace together. Baste the edge of the lace to the outer edge, on the right side of the embroidery, placing the bound edge of the lace just inside the 12mm (½in) seam allowance and lying on the fabric. Allow a little extra fullness at the corners. Machine stitch in place.

With right sides together, place the backing fabric on top. Baste and machine stitch around the edges, leaving a 20cm (8in) opening in the middle of one side. Remove the basting; trim across the corners, and turn the cover to the right side. Insert the cushion pad; turn in the edges of the opening, and slipstitch to close.

△ 3064 brown (bks 839)
✠ 839 dark brown
◣ 415 grey (and bks 414*)

● 310 black
*Note: 3 additional
backstitch colours*

S  676 straw (and
   bks 780*)
I  948 flesh (and
   bks 352*)
◣  927 drab
   tuquoise
   (bks 924)
●  800 blue
↓  3364 green
△  3362 drab green
○  924 dark green
   (and bks
   3371*)
⊡  435 light brown
   (bks eyebrow)
✱  611 brown
◆  415 grey
   *Note: 3
   additional
   backstitch
   colours*

# LITTLE BO-PEEP

## YOU WILL NEED

For a cushion measuring 35cm (14in) square:

*40cm (16in) square of cream evenweave (Aida)*
*fabric, 16 threads to 2.5cm (1in)*
*38cm (15in) square of contrast floral print for*
*the backing; 12mm (¹/₂in) seam allowances*
*are included*
*250cm (2²/₃yds) of cream lace trim;*
*4cm (1¹/₂in) wide*
*DMC stranded embroidery cotton in the colours*
*given in the panel*
*No 26 tapestry needle*
*Matching sewing thread*
*38cm (15in) square cushion pad*

●

## THE EMBROIDERY

Prepare the fabric and stretch it in an embroidery frame, following the instructions given on page 121. Referring to the chart, complete the cross stitching, using two strands of thread in the needle. Work the backstitching on top, using a single strand of thread. Take the embroidery out of the frame and steam press it on the wrong side.

## MAKING UP THE CUSHION

Trim the embroidery to 38cm (15in) square, as for the Ride a cock-horse cushion, see page 112.

Using a tiny french seam, join the short edges of the lace together. Run a gathering thread close to the straight edge. Pull up the gathers to fit, and with the right side of the embroidery facing and the lace lying on the fabric, baste the edging to the outer edge, placing it just inside the seam allowance. Adjust the gathers evenly, allowing a little extra fullness at the corners. Machine stitch in place.

Place the backing fabric on top, right sides together; baste and machine stitch around, leaving a 20cm (8in) opening in the middle of one side. Take out the basting; trim across the corners, and turn the cover through. Insert the cushion pad and slipstitch the opening to secure.

# 𝒜LPHABET

A beautifully designed alphabet has many uses in cross stitch embroidery. It can be stitched *en bloc* as a patchwork motif for a child's quilt, for example, or individual letters can be embroidered on separate patches. Alternatively, the letters can be adapted to spell out a greeting on a card or a birth quilt, or incorporated into a design for a cushion or a small picture to commemorate a special occasion, such as a wedding or a birthday.

Gifts can be personalized by adding initials or a name, or you can even make a traditional alphabet sampler, also utilizing border designs from pages 118 or taking motifs from other projects in this book and repeating them to make patterns.

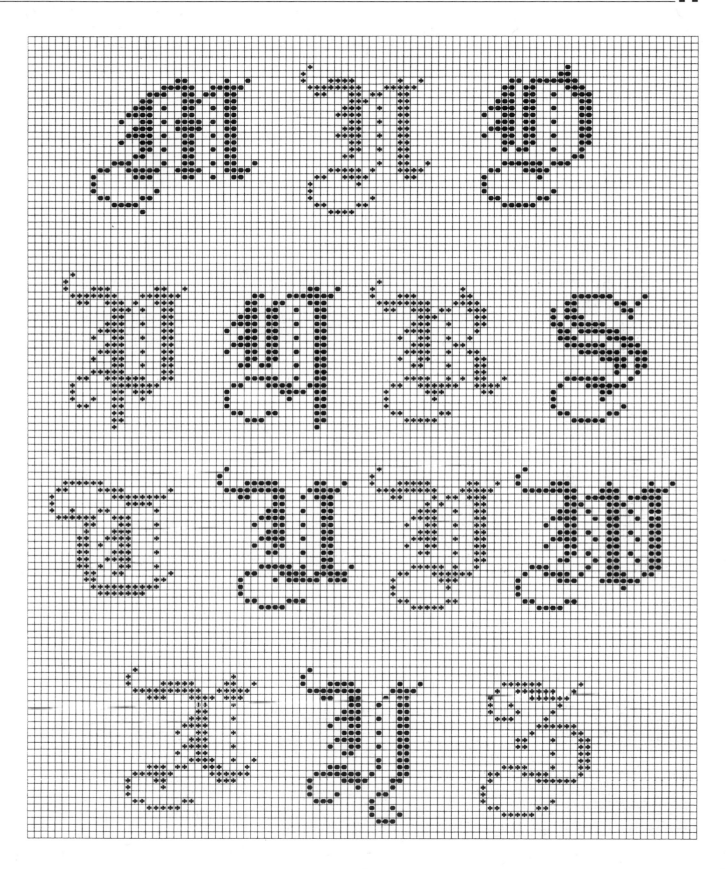

# BORDER DESIGNS

A well-chosen border will give a finishing touch to your embroidery that can be as simple or as complex as you like. The selection given here is purely inspirational, but any of these could easily be copied or adapted to suit your own design ideas.

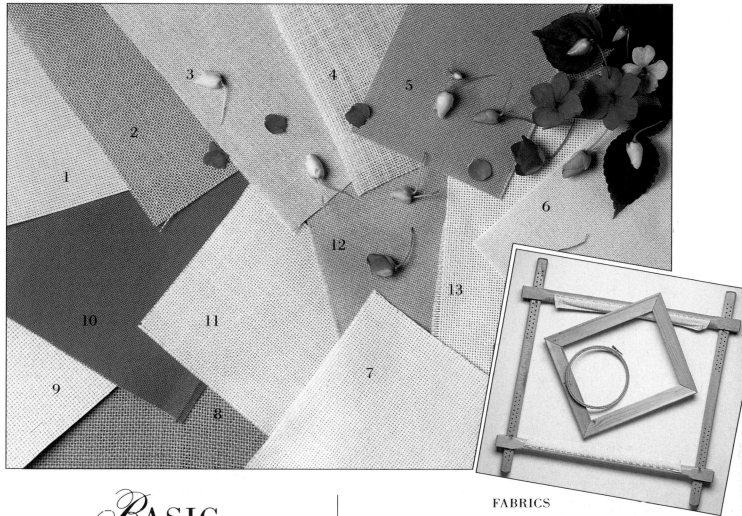

# $\mathscr{B}$ASIC EQUIPMENT

The basic equipment needed for cross stitching is moderately simple and can be bought at most department stores or needlework suppliers. In fact, when you begin to collect the items together, you will probably find that you already have most of them in your workbox and around the home.

*1 16 count Aida; 2 24ct linen; 3 30ct linen; 4 20ct linen; 5 25ct Linda; 6 27ct Linda; 7 16ct Hardanger; 8 16ct linen; 9 14ct Aida; 10 28ct cotton; 11 18ct wool; 12 18ct Ainring; 13 18ct Davosa.*

## FABRICS

For best results, cross stitch is worked on an even-weave fabric. This is any fabric with the same number of threads counted in both directions over, for example, 2.5cm (1in).

Traditionally, cross stitch embroidery is worked on linen, which often has a charming hand-woven finish. Although they are not now produced in the variety and quantities of former years and those that are available tend to be expensive, linens in a limited range of weights and colours – including Hardanger and huckaback types – can be brought from specialist suppliers. Whereas ordinary linens have a single weave, Hardanger has a double weave, and huckaback is woven in groups of threads to form a checked pattern.

In addition to linens, many other evenweaves are available, some made from cotton and others from a blend of synthetic and cotton fibres. These fabrics include Zweigart's Aida and Tula, which are woven with groups of threads and have a pronounced checked effect. They are produced in different weights and many colours. Zweigart's Lugana and Linda have a single weave and are also available in a range of weights and colours.

Aida and some other cotton fabrics can be quite stiff to handle, due to the fact that they are finished with a fairly heavy dressing. This will wash out to a certain extent, and although the stiffened fabric will help to give the embroidery an even tension, you may prefer to hand wash the fabric beforehand.

## THREADS

Different types of thread can be used for cross stitch embroidery but, for the purposes of this book, stranded embroidery cotton has been used throughout. The number of strands required for each project is given with the instructions. As a general rule, however, the thickness of the embroidery thread should match the weight of the fabric. And for best results, the aim should be to have clearly defined stitches which cover the fabric well and give a sharpness to the overall design.

## NEEDLES

For cross stitching on evenweave fabric, use round-ended tapestry needles. You will find that these move easily between the intersections of the fabric without piercing the ground threads. Tapestry needles are available in sizes ranging from 18–26.

When finishing the projects, a selection of sharps is required for hand sewing, and for quilting, either quilting needles or betweens are recommended.

## FRAMES

Depending on the size of the embroidery and the amount of cross stitching involved, either a rectangular frame or a hoop of the appropriate size can be used to support the fabric while stitching.

Although a frame is not an absolute essential, there are positive advantages to using one. Firstly, it will keep the fabric evenly stretched and prevent it from becoming distorted. This can easily happen when working with fabric in the hand, especially if the stitch is made by 'scooping' the fabric.

Secondly, if the frame is supported, this leaves both hands free to stitch. With one hand on top and the other below, the correct up and down move-

ments can be used and, with practice, you will find that you can work quicker this way.

## SCISSORS

In all fabric crafts it is essential to keep the right type of scissors for the job. For cutting out, use sharp dressmaker's shears and, to prevent the blades from becoming blunt, do not allow them to be used for other tasks. For snipping into seams and cutting threads, a pair of sharp-pointed small embroidery scissors are needed. It is also a good idea to have a pair of general-purpose scissors for cutting paper, card, cord and so on.

## SEWING MACHINE

A sewing machine should be used for all making-up purposes where seaming is involved, especially on large items such as quilts and cushion covers. You will not need an elaborate machine to make up the projects in this book. All that is required is that it stitches reliably, gives a good straight stitch and, ideally, has a reverse stitch for convenience when starting and finishing.

## IRON

This is one of the most important pieces of equipment required for any fabric craft. A thermostatically controlled steam iron gives excellent results and is particularly good for this type of embroidery, for pressing seams, and for general ironing.

When making up projects, always keep your iron and board to hand so that you can 'press as you sew' to get the very best finish.

## GENERAL ACCESSORIES

In addition to the items already mentioned; you will require a good supply of dressmaker's stainless steel pins, a measuring tape, basting thread, ruler and pencil.

While a thimble is not necessarily used for embroidery, it is a good idea to use one for general sewing purposes, especially for hand-sewing through bulky seams. For all kinds of quilting, you will find that one, if not two, thimbles are essential. Here, the second thimble is worn on the first or second finger of the hand that works below the frame as it guides the needle back through the fabric.

# Basic Skills

The basic skills required for making the projects in the book can be found in the following pages.

### PREPARING THE FABRIC

Unless fabrics have been stored unfolded on a roll, they will probably be creased, especially along the centre. Before cutting out, therefore, steam press all fabrics to remove any creases. When cutting out main sections, try to be as economical as possible, cutting on the grainline to avoid wastage.

Even with an average amount of handling, many evenweave fabrics tend to fray at the edges, so it is a good idea to overcast the raw edges, using ordinary sewing thread, before embroidering. When calculating quantities, always allow extra fabric to account for the possibility of fraying.

### WORKING IN A HOOP

A hoop is the most popular frame for use with small areas of embroidery. It consists of two rings, one fitted inside the other; the outer ring usually has an adjustable screw attachment so that it can be tightened to hold the stretched fabric in place. Hoops are available in several sizes, ranging from 10cm (4in) in diameter to quilting hoops with a diameter of 38cm (15in). Hoops with table stands or floor stands attached are also available.

**1** To stretch your fabric in a hoop, place the area to be embroidered over the inner ring and press the outer ring over it, with the tension screw released.

**2** Smooth the fabric and, if needed, straighten the grain before tightening the screw. The fabric should be evenly stretched.

**3** Tissue paper can be placed between the outer ring and the embroidery, so that the hoop does not mark the fabric. Tear away the paper as shown.

### WORKING IN A RECTANGULAR FRAME

Rectangular frames consist of two rollers, with tapes attached, and two flat side pieces, which slot into the rollers and are held in place by pegs or screw attachments. They are measured by the length of the roller tape, and range in size from 30cm (12in) to 68cm (27in). As alternatives to a slate frame, canvas stretchers and the backs of old picture frames can be used.

**1** To stretch your fabric in a rectangular frame, cut out the fabric, allowing at least an extra 5cm (2in)

all around the finished size of the embroidery. Baste a single 12mm (½in) turning on the top and bottom edges and oversew strong tape, 2.5cm (1in) wide, to the other two sides. Mark the centre line both ways with basting stitches.

**2** Working from the centre outwards and using strong thread, oversew the top and bottom edges to the roller tapes. Fit the side pieces into the slots, and roll any extra fabric on one roller until the fabric is taut.

**3** Insert the pegs or adjust the screw attachments to secure the frame. Thread a large-eyed needle (chenille needle) with strong thread or fine string and lace both edges, securing the ends around the intersections of the frame. Lace the webbing at 2.5cm (1in) intervals, stretching the fabric evenly.

### ENLARGING A GRAPH PATTERN

One or two graph patterns are given in this book. These must be enlarged to the correct size. The scale of the full-size pattern is given on the appropriate page; for example, 'Each square = 5cm (2in)' means that each small square on the printed diagram should correspond to a 5cm (2in) square on your enlarged grid.

1 square = 2.5cm (1in)

● To enlarge a graph pattern, you will need a sheet of graph paper ruled in 1cm (⅜in) squares, a ruler and pencil. If, for example, the scale is one square to 5cm (2in) you should first mark the appropriate lines to give a grid of the correct size. Copy the graph freehand from the small grid to the larger one, completing one square at a time. Use a ruler to draw the straight lines first, and then copy the freehand curves.

### BIAS BINDING

As its name suggests, bias binding is cut across the grain to allow the most 'give', and is an excellent binding for all edges, especially curves.

It is available in three sizes: 12mm (½in), 2.5cm (1in) and 5cm (2in), and in a wonderful variety of colours. Cotton lawn is by far the most popular and practical type, although satins and synthetic mixes are also available. Two methods of binding an edge are shown here; in the first, the binding is attached by stitching through all layers, while in the second it is attached in two stages, so that the stitching cannot be seen on the right side of the fabric.

● Using double-fold bias binding, encase the raw edge with binding and baste in place. Working from the right side, machine stitch along the edge so that both sides are stitched at the same time.

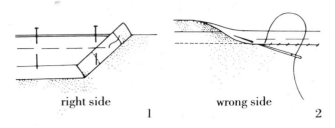

right side        wrong side

1                  2

**1** Alternatively, open out the turning on one edge of the binding and pin in position on the right side of the fabric, matching the fold to the seamline. Fold over the cut end of the binding. Finish by overlapping the starting point by about 12mm (½in). Pin, baste and machine stitch to cover the seamline.

**2** Fold the binding over the raw edge to the wrong side, baste and, using matching sewing thread, neatly hem to finish.

### PIPED SEAMS

Contrasting piping adds a special decorative finish to a seam and looks particularly attractive on items such as cushions and cosies.

You can cover piping cord with either bias-cut fabric of your choice or a bias binding; alternatively, ready-covered piping cord is available in several widths and many colours.

**1** To apply piping, pin, baste and stitch it to the right side of the fabric, with seam lines matching. Clip into the seam allowance where necessary.

**2** With right sides together, place the second piece of fabric on top, enclosing the piping. Baste and then either hand stitch in place or machine stitch, using a zipper foot. Stitch as close to the piping as possible, covering the first line of stitching

**3** To join ends of piping together, first overlap the two ends by about 2.5cm (1in). Unpick the two cut ends of bias to reveal the cord. Join the bias strip as shown. Trim and press the seam open. Unravel the cord, and splice the two ends. Fold the bias strip over the cord, and finish basting around the edge.

### MITRING CORNERS

There are several types of mitre, but in each case the purpose is essentially to reduce bulk and to make the corner neat and square.

**1** To mitre a corner, first plan the depth of the hem and allow an extra 6mm (¼in) for turning. Fold over the corner as shown in the diagram and finger-press the creaseline.

**2** Allow a further 6mm (¼in) beyond this line and cut across.

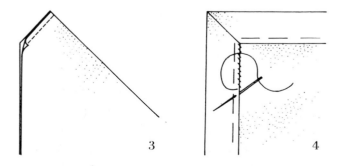

**3** Fold the fabric with the two outer edges together and machine stitch across, taking a 6mm (¼in) seam and stopping at the creased line of the hem.

**4** Press the seam open and turn the corner to the right side. Either turn under the hem, baste and hem on the wrong side or, if you are hemstitching, work on the right side, following the instructions given with the project.

### ATTACHING A CORD

A twisted cord in plain or mixed colours gives a pretty finish to a cushion. Cords are available in wool, cotton, silk and synthetic fibres and in a great variety of colours and thicknesses.

seam

● To attach a cord, simply slip one cut end into the seam and secure with matching thread. Slipstitch the cord around the edge of the cushion, alternately catching the underside of the cord only and sliding the needle under the seam so that the finished stitching is completely hidden.
Finish with the two ends just overlapped, neatly tucked into the seam and firmly secured.

### MOUNTING EMBROIDERY

Embroidered pictures and other similar projects look best if they are first stretched over cardboard before framing. Very lightweight fabrics can be attached at the back with pieces of masking tape, but heavier fabrics are best laced across the back.

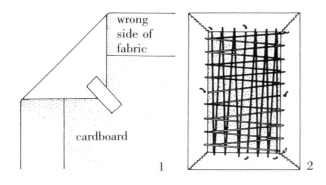

wrong side of fabric

cardboard

1               2

**1** The cardboard should be cut to the size of the finished embroidery, with an extra 6mm (¼in)

added all around to allow for the recess in the picture frame.

**2** With the embroidery face down and the cardboard centred over it, fold over the edges of the fabric on opposite sides and lace across, using strong thread. Repeat on the other two sides, first folding each corner into a mitre. Finally, pull up the stitches fairly tightly to stretch the fabric firmly over the cardboard. Overstitch the mitred corners.

### SEAMS

Unless otherwise stated, all seams are straight seams, with a 12mm (½in) seam allowance, pressed open to finish. In some cases, a french seam is specified. To make this, place the two fabrics with wrong sides together and join them with a narrow seam. Press the seam to one side, and turn the two pieces so that the wrong sides are now facing outwards. Make a second seam enclosing the first.

### CROSS STITCH

For all cross stitch embroidery, the following two methods of working are used. In each case, neat rows of vertical stitches are produced on the back of the fabric.

1

2

**1** When stitching large areas, work in horizontal rows. Working from right to left, complete the first row of evenly spaced diagonal stitches over the number of threads specified in the project instructions. Then, working from left to right, repeat the process. Continue in this way, making sure each stitch and successive rows cross in the same direction throughout.

**2** When stitching diagonal lines, work downwards, completing each stitch before moving to the next.

### HEMSTITCH

This stitch is the traditional way of finishing the hems of embroidered napkins and tablecloths. For a fringed hem, remove a single thread at the hem and stitch along the line as shown. When you have finished, remove the weft threads below the hem-stitching, to make a fringe.

To secure a hem that has been turned up to the drawn-thread line and basted, hemstitch as shown, but at the second stage of each stitch ensure that the needle pierces the hem at the back of the fabric before you pull the thread through, ready to repeat the stitch along the line.

*Note* When hemstitching Aida and similar fabrics, it is not necessary to remove the initial thread, as the lines between blocks are clearly distinguished; the stitches can be worked along a line of blocks or groups of threads. As you are stitching blocks instead of single threads, make sure that you refer to the project instructions to discover the number of blocks to work for the hemstitching.

Bring the needle out on the right side, two threads below the drawn-thread line. Working from left to right, pick up either two or three threads, as shown in the diagram. Bring the needle out again and insert it behind the fabric, to emerge two threads down, ready to make the next stitch. Before reinserting the needle, pull the thread tight, so that the bound threads form a neat group

### BACKSTITCH

Backstitch is used in the projects to give emphasis to a particular foldline, an outline or a shadow. The stitches are worked over the same number of threads as the cross stitch, forming continuous straight or diagonal lines.

● Make the first stitch from left to right; pass the needle behind the fabric, and bring it out one stitch length ahead to the left. Repeat and continue in this way along the line.

### STAR EYELET

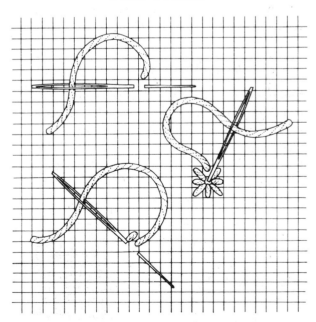

Beginning at the top right corner, work eight straight stitches over two threads (the length of the particular cross stitch being worked), working from the outer edge into the centre, as shown in the diagram.

# CONVERSION CHART

Not all of these colour conversions are exact matches, and bracketed
numbers are given as close substitutes.

| DMC | ANCHOR | COATS | MADEIRA | DMC | ANCHOR | COATS | MADEIRA | DMC | ANCHOR | COATS | MADEIRA |
|-----|--------|-------|---------|-----|--------|-------|---------|-----|--------|-------|---------|
| White | 2 | 1001 | White | 434 | 309 | 5000 | 2009 | 721 | (324) | 2329 | 0308 |
| 208 | (110) | 4301 | 0804 | 435 | (365) | 5371 | 2010 | 722 | (323) | 2099 | 0307 |
| 209 | 105 | 4302 | 0803 | 436 | (363) | 5943 | 2011 | 725 | (306) | 2298 | 0108 |
| 210 | 104 | 4303 | 0802 | 437 | 362 | 5942 | 2012 | 726 | 295 | 2294 | 0109 |
| 213 | 895 | — | 0812 | 444 | 291 | 2298 | 0108 | 727 | 293 | — | 0110 |
| 221 | (897) | 3242 | 0811 | 445 | 288 | — | 0103 | 734 | (279) | — | 1610 |
| 224 | 893 | 3241 | 0813 | 469 | 267 | — | 1503 | 738 | 942 | 5375 | 2013 |
| 225 | 892 | 3006 | 0814 | 471 | (280) | — | 1501 | 739 | (366) | 5369 | 2014 |
| 300 | (352) | — | 2304 | 498 | (47) | — | 0511 | 740 | 316 | 2099 | 0202 |
| 301 | (349) | — | 2306 | 517 | (162) | — | 1107 | 741 | 304 | 2314 | 0201 |
| 304 | (47) | 3401 | 0509 | 535 | (401) | 8400 | 1809 | 742 | 303 | 2303 | 0114 |
| 307 | (289) | 2290 | 0104 | 550 | (101) | 4107 | 0714 | 743 | (297) | 2302 | 0113 |
| 309 | (42) | 3284 | 0507 | 552 | 100 | 4092 | 0713 | 744 | (301) | 2293 | 0112 |
| 310 | 403 | 8403 | Black | 553 | 98 | 4097 | 0712 | 745 | (300) | 2296 | 0111 |
| 311 | 148 | — | 1006 | 554 | (96) | 4104 | 0711 | 746 | (386) | — | 0101 |
| 312 | (147) | 7979 | 1005 | 564 | 203 | — | 1208 | 754 | (6) | 2331 | 0305 |
| 317 | (400) | 8512 | 1714 | 597 | (168) | — | 1110 | 758 | 868 | 2337 | 0403 |
| 318 | (399) | 8511 | 1802 | 602 | (63) | 3063 | 0702 | 760 | (9) | 3069 | 0405 |
| 319 | (246) | 6246 | 1313 | 603 | (62) | 3001 | 0701 | 761 | (8) | 3068 | 0404 |
| 320 | (216) | 6017 | 1311 | 605 | (50) | 3151 | 0613 | 762 | 397 | 8510 | 1804 |
| 321 | 47 | 3500 | 0510 | 606 | 335 | 2334 | 0209 | 772 | (264) | 6250 | 1604 |
| 322 | (978) | 7978 | 1004 | 608 | (333) | 2332 | 0206 | 776 | (24) | 3281 | 0503 |
| 326 | (59) | 3401 | 0508 | 610 | 906 | — | 2106 | 778 | (968) | — | 0808 |
| 333 | 119 | — | 0903 | 611 | 898 | — | 2107 | 780 | 309 | — | 2214 |
| 334 | 161 | 7977 | 1003 | 612 | 832 | — | 2108 | 781 | 308 | — | 2213 |
| 335 | (42) | 3283 | 0506 | 613 | 831 | — | 2109 | 782 | 307 | — | 2212 |
| 340 | 118 | 7110 | 0902 | 632 | (936) | — | 2311 | 783 | 307 | — | 2211 |
| 341 | 117 | — | 0901 | 640 | 903 | 5393 | 1905 | 791 | 941 | — | 0904 |
| 347 | (19) | 3013 | 0407 | 642 | 392 | — | 1906 | 792 | 941 | 7150 | 0905 |
| 349 | 13 | 2335 | 0212 | 644 | 830 | 8501 | 1907 | 793 | 121 | 721 | 0906 |
| 350 | (11) | 3011 | 0213 | 645 | (400) | 8500 | 1811 | 794 | 120 | — | 0907 |
| 351 | (10) | 3012 | 0214 | 647 | (8581) | 8900 | 1813 | 796 | (133) | 7100 | 0913 |
| 352 | (9) | 3008 | 0303 | 648 | 900 | 8390 | 1814 | 797 | (132) | 7023 | 0912 |
| 353 | (8) | 3006 | 0304 | 666 | 46 | 3046 | 0210 | 798 | (131) | 7022 | 0911 |
| 355 | 5968 | 2339 | 0401 | 676 | 891 | 2305 | 2208 | 799 | (130) | 7030 | 0910 |
| 367 | (262) | 6018 | 1312 | 677 | (886) | 2300 | 2207 | 800 | (128) | — | 0908 |
| 368 | (261) | 6016 | 1310 | 680 | 901 | 5374 | 2210 | 801 | (357) | 5475 | 2007 |
| 371 | (856) | — | 2111 | 699 | (923) | 6228 | 1303 | 806 | (169) | — | 1108 |
| 402 | (347) | — | 2307 | 700 | 229 | 6227 | 1304 | 807 | (168) | — | 1109 |
| 407 | (882) | — | 2310 | 701 | 227 | 6226 | 1305 | 809 | (130) | 7021 | 0909 |
| 413 | 401 | 8514 | 1713 | 702 | 226 | 6239 | 1306 | 813 | (160) | — | 1013 |
| 414 | (400) | 8513 | 1801 | 703 | 238 | 6238 | 1307 | 814 | (44) | — | 0514 |
| 415 | 398 | 8510 | 1803 | 704 | (256) | 6238 | 1308 | 815 | 43 | 3000 | 0513 |
| 420 | (375) | 5374 | 2104 | 712 | (387) | 5387 | 2101 | 816 | (20) | 3410 | 0512 |
| 422 | (373) | 5372 | 2102 | 718 | 88 | — | 0707 | 817 | 47 | 2335 | 0211 |
| 433 | (371) | 5471 | 2008 | 720 | (326) | — | 0309 | 818 | 48 | 3281 | 0502 |

| DMC | ANCHOR | COATS | MADEIRA | DMC | ANCHOR | COATS | MADEIRA | DMC | ANCHOR | COATS | MADEIRA |
|---|---|---|---|---|---|---|---|---|---|---|---|
| 819 | (892) | 3280 | 0501 | 943 | 188 | — | 1203 | 3078 | 292 | 2292 | 0102 |
| 822 | (390) | 5387 | 1908 | 945 | 881 | — | 2313 | 3325 | (159) | 7976 | 1002 |
| 823 | 150 | — | 1008 | 946 | 332 | — | 0207 | 3326 | (26) | 3126 | 0504 |
| 824 | (164) | — | 1010 | 947 | (330) | 2327 | 0205 | 3328 | (11) | 3071 | 0408 |
| 825 | (162) | — | 1011 | 948 | (778) | 2331 | 0306 | 3345 | (268) | 6258 | 1406 |
| 826 | (161) | — | 1012 | 950 | 4146 | — | 2309 | 3346 | (257) | 6258 | 1407 |
| 827 | (159) | — | 1014 | 951 | (880) | — | 2308 | 3347 | (267) | 6266 | 1408 |
| 828 | (158) | — | 1101 | 954 | 204 | — | 1211 | 3348 | 265 | 6266 | 1409 |
| 829 | (906) | — | 2113 | 955 | 203 | — | 1210 | 3350 | 69 | — | 0603 |
| 833 | 907 | — | 2114 | 956 | 54 | — | 0611 | 3354 | (75) | — | 0608 |
| 834 | 874 | — | 2204 | 957 | 52 | — | 0612 | 3364 | (843) | 6010 | 1603 |
| 838 | 380 | 7982 | 1914 | 958 | 187 | 6186 | 1114 | 3371 | 382 | — | 2004 |
| 840 | (379) | 5379 | 1912 | 959 | 186 | 6185 | 1113 | 3607 | (87) | — | 0708 |
| 841 | (378) | 5376 | 1911 | 961 | 40 | — | 0610 | 3608 | 86 | — | 0709 |
| 842 | 376 | — | 1910 | 962 | 52 | — | 0609 | 3609 | (85) | — | 0710 |
| 844 | 401 | — | 1810 | 963 | 48 | — | 0608 | 3685 | (70) | — | 0602 |
| 869 | (944) | — | 2105 | 966 | 206 | — | 1209 | 3687 | (68) | — | 0604 |
| 890 | (218) | 6021 | 1314 | 970 | (316) | 2327 | 0204 | 3688 | (66) | — | 0605 |
| 891 | 29 | — | 0411 | 971 | (316) | 2099 | 0203 | 3689 | 73 | — | 0607 |
| 892 | 28 | — | 0412 | 972 | 303 | — | 0107 | 3705 | (35) | — | 0410 |
| 893 | 27 | — | 0413 | 973 | 297 | — | 0105 | 3706 | (33) | — | 0409 |
| 894 | 26 | — | 0414 | 975 | 352 | — | 2303 | 3708 | (31) | — | 0408 |
| 898 | 360 | 5476 | 2006 | 976 | (309) | — | 2302 | 3712 | 10 | — | — |
| 899 | (27) | 3282 | 0505 | 977 | (307) | 2306 | 2301 | 3731 | 76 | — | — |
| 902 | (72) | 3083 | 0601 | 986 | (246) | 6021 | 1404 | 3733 | 75 | — | — |
| 904 | (258) | 6258 | 1413 | 987 | (245) | 6258 | 1403 | 3756 | 158 | — | — |
| 906 | (256) | 6256 | 1411 | 988 | (257) | 6258 | 1402 | 3761 | 159 | — | — |
| 910 | (228) | 6031 | 1301 | 989 | (256) | 6266 | 1401 | 3766 | 167 | — | — |
| 911 | (205) | 6205 | 1214 | 991 | 212 | — | 1204 | 3774 | 778 | — | — |
| 912 | 209 | 6225 | 1212 | 992 | (187) | 6186 | 1202 | 3779 | 4146 | — | — |
| 919 | (341) | 2326 | 0314 | 993 | (186) | — | 1201 | | | | |
| 920 | (339) | 3337 | 0312 | 995 | 410 | 7010 | 1102 | | | | |
| 921 | (338) | 2326 | 0311 | 996 | 433 | 7001 | 1103 | | | | |
| 922 | (324) | 3336 | 0310 | 3011 | 856 | — | 1607 | | | | |
| 924 | (851) | 6008 | 1706 | 3021 | (382) | 5395 | 1904 | | | | |
| 926 | (779) | 6007 | 1707 | 3022 | (8581) | — | 1903 | | | | |
| 927 | (849) | 6006 | 1708 | 3024 | (391) | 8390 | 1901 | | | | |
| 928 | (900) | 7225 | 1709 | 3031 | (905) | 5472 | 2003 | | | | |
| 930 | (922) | 7052 | 1712 | 3033 | 387 | — | 2001 | | | | |
| 931 | (921) | 7051 | 1711 | 3042 | 869 | 4221 | 0807 | | | | |
| 932 | (920) | 7050 | 1710 | 3045 | (888) | — | 2103 | | | | |
| 935 | 862 | — | 1505 | 3046 | (887) | 2410 | 2206 | | | | |
| 936 | 269 | — | 1507 | 3047 | (886) | 2300 | 2205 | | | | |
| 937 | 268 | — | 1504 | 3051 | (846) | — | 1508 | | | | |
| 938 | 381 | — | 2005 | 3052 | (844) | — | 1509 | | | | |
| 939 | 152 | — | 1009 | 3053 | (859) | 6315 | 1510 | | | | |

# INDEX

A cat came fiddling  95
A child's picture  87
A frog he would a-wooing go  35
A little man  62
Afternoon-tea cloth  55
Alphabet  116

Baa-baa black sheep  15
Basic equipment  119
Basic skills  121
Birthday greetings cards  62
Border designs  118
Bordered pictures  90
Butterfly, butterfly  19

Carriage clock  80
Christmas greetings cards  83
Coffee and tea  75
Coffee-pot cosy  76
Coffee-pot stand  79
Come out to play  11
Corded cushion  27
Curly-locks  107

Dame get up  83
Drinks tray  11

Friday night's dream  38
Fringed guest towel  95
Fringed place mats and napkins  22

Hickety, pickety  22
Hickory, dickory, dock  75
Hot cross buns  38
Humpty Dumpty  22

Jack and Jill  90
Jack be nimble  38
Jack Sprat  38

I had a little nut tree  27
I saw three ships  83

Lace-edged cushions  110
Lacy lavender sachets  19
Lavender blue  19
Little Bo-peep  110
Little boy blue  103
Little disaster  87
Little Jack Horner  83
Little maid  38
Little maid, pretty maid  67
Little maiden  70
Lucy Locket  38

Magpie, magpie  30
Mary, Mary, quite contrary  19
Mary's canary  30
Miniature pictures  67
Miss Muffet  62

Nightdress case  15
Nursery-rhyme patchwork quilt  38

Pease pudding  38
Pippin Hill  38
Polly put the kettle on  75
Pretty pincushions  70

Quite well, quite hearty  67

Ride a cock-horse  38, 110
Ring-a-ring-a-roses  38
Rock-a-bye, baby  67

Sleep baby, sleep  107

Tea-time tray  35
The cat and the fiddle  55
The lion and the unicorn  99
The rose is red  19
The ten o'clock scholar  30
This little pig  62
Tied-on pillow cover  103
Tom, Tom, the piper's son  90
Tommy Tittlemouse  38, 90
Traditional dressing-table set  107
Trim bookmarks  30
Twinkle, twinkle, little star  107
Two birds  70

You shall have an apple  38

Victorian-style footstool  99

Wee Willie Winkie  70

# SUPPLIERS

The following mail order companies have supplied some of the basic items needed for making up the projects in this book:

*United Kingdom*
Remember When
Cheriton Cottage
Wreningham
Norwich NR16 1BE. England.

Framecraft Miniatures Limited
148-150 High Street
Aston
Birmingham B6 4US. England.
Telephone (021) 359 4442

*Addresses for Framecraft worldwide*
Ireland Needlecraft Pty. Ltd.
2-4 Keppel Drive
Hallam
Victoria 3803
Australia

Danish Art Needlework
PO Box 442
Lethbridge
Alberta T1J 3Z1
Canada

Sanyei Imports
PO Box 5
Hashima Shi
Gifu 501-62
Japan

The Embroidery Shop
286 Queen Street
Masterton
New Zealand

Anne Brinkley Designs Inc.
246 Walnut Street
Newton
Mass. 02160
USA

S A Threads and Cottons Ltd.
43 Somerset Road
Cape Town
South Africa